# THE MAGIC LENS



## LEVEL 1

### STUDENT EDITION

### REVISED & EXPANDED

by
**Michael Clay Thompson**

**Royal Fireworks Press**
**Unionville, New York**

Royal Fireworks Press
First Avenue, PO Box 399
Unionville, NY 10988-0399
TEL: (845) 726-4444
FAX: (845) 726-3824
email: rfpress@frontiernet.net

ISBN: 0-88092-210-9

Printed in the United States of America on acid-free, recycled paper
using soy-based inks by the Royal Fireworks Printing Company
of Unionville, New York.

# Table of Contents


Grammar: A Way of Thinking about Language . . . . . 1

1 Parts of Speech . . . . . 5

2 Parts of the Sentence . . . . . 51

3 Phrases . . . . . 66

4 Clauses . . . . . 79

Common English Grammar & Usage Problems . . . . . 97

Solecism Theatre . . . . . 102

Loop 1 . . . . . 106

Loop 2 . . . . . 117

Loop 3 . . . . . 128

Loop 4 . . . . . 139

Loop 5 . . . . . 150

Loop 6 . . . . . 163

Loop 7 . . . . . 174

Loop 8 . . . . . 185

Loop 9 . . . . . 196

Loop 10 . . . . . 207

By degrees I made a discovery of still greater moment. I found that these people possessed a method of communicating their experience and feelings to one another by articulate sounds. I perceived that the words they spoke sometimes, produced pleasure or pain, smiles or sadness, in the minds and countenances of the hearers. This was indeed a godlike science, and I ardently desired to become acquainted with it.

-The monster, in Mary Shelley's *Frankenstein*

# Grammar

A way of thinking about language.

## A Way of Thinking About Language

**Grammar**: Like formal logic, grammar is a method of critical thinking. It allows us to build good sentences that are consistent and logically valid. It lets sentences contain truth. It allows us to identify and extirpate ambiguities and internal disagreements from our thought. Grammar reveals to us that each thought is a *paradigm of simplicity*, a two-part structure, made of a subject and a predicate about the subject. The form of a thought is:

Grammar shows us the parts of thoughts' subjects, and the parts of thoughts' predicates. Grammar shows us how to simplify thoughts, how to combine thoughts that are aspects of one another, and how to modify thoughts until they are precise. Grammar shows us how to express the truth, and how to avoid contradicting what we have already said. Grammar is a set of principles and reflections about thoughts, and with these reflections, you can think.

We can express some of these ideas succinctly by saying that **grammar is a way of thinking about language**.

**Grammar is<br>a way<br>of thinking about language.**

Grammar lets us think about language by giving us names for different kinds of words and for the different ways that words represent our thoughts and feelings.

Grammar is a small subject with a few, high-precision concepts, and we will see that most terms in grammar are so beautifully named, they are self-defining.

Without grammar, we can't discuss language problems, compare writing styles, or resolve language dilemmas, and it is also more difficult to sort ideas into clear and distinct groups of words. For these reasons, grammar is fascinating and worthwhile.

**p** as ***f*** of **G**

**Punctuation Is a Function of Grammar**: Punctuation is the art of marking the four levels of grammar so that written ideas and parts of ideas do not become confusing. In other words, when we punctuate, we *separate the groups of grammar from each other*. Since it is grammar we punctuate, it is impossible to punctuate unless we first see the grammatical structures, such as phrases, dependent clauses, and compound sentences. You cannot punctuate a *nonessential adjective clause* if you don't know it's there.

4

**Four Levels of Grammar:** We do grammar in **four approaches** or levels. They are the **parts of speech**, **parts of the sentence**, **phrases**, and **clauses**. When we analyze the grammar of a sentence, that is what we do: a four-level analysis.

Grammar: **Four** Levels

**1**. Parts of speech
**2**. Parts of the sentence
**3**. Phrases
**4**. Clauses

These four levels give us four different views of each sentence. The **parts of speech** level shows us each word, one at a time, asking "What is this word doing?" The **parts of sentence** level shows us the architecture of the idea, asking, "What is being said about what?" The **phrases** level shows us the little groups of words in the sentence, groups that pretend to be a single part of speech, asking "What part of speech is this group of words doing?" And the **clauses** level shows us whether or not more than one idea is drawn into the sentence's design, asking "How many different ideas are connected together in this sentence?" Although we will explain the details of this four-level analysis later, we can demonstrate the simplicity of the four levels by looking at a sentence from poet T.S. Eliot:

| | **These** | **fragments** | **I** | **have** | **shored** | **against** | **my** | **ruins.** |
|---|---|---|---|---|---|---|---|---|
| **Parts of Speech:** | adj. | n. | pron. | v. | v. | prep. | pron. | n. |
| **Parts of Sentence:** | ---- direct object--- | | subj. | ------pred.----- | | | | |
| **Phrases:** | | | | | | --prepositional phrase-- | | |
| **Clauses:** | ---------one independent clause, simple declarative sentence-------- | | | | | | | |

**Level?** Before we continue, consider for a moment that the word ***level*** is a strata metaphor. In looking at the parts of speech, parts of the sentence, phrases, and clauses of a sentence, we are *thinking about the same sentence in four different ways*; we are examining four different phenomena within the sentence. Rather than four levels of depth, our four different views are really more like four different views of the same human body, which looks different in visible light, x-rays, infrared images, and CAT-scans. There is only one sentence; it is we who are looking through it, thinking and then rethinking about it four different times.

## It's not so much to learn.

**A Term Total**: If you have ever had the sinking feeling that grammar is an endless subject, you should notice a secret (shhhhh): most grammar books are thick only because they are padded with *hundreds of pages of exercises*. The actual content of grammar is tiny. It is *very* learnable. In fact, sixty or so terms are all you really have to know to be unusually competent in your essential grammar, and there are only about twenty key terms! Here are most of the grammar terms you need, with the key terms in bold:

### A Term Total

| PARTS OF SPEECH | PARTS OF SENTENCE | PHRASES | CLAUSES |
|---|---|---|---|
| **noun** | sentence | phrase | **independent** |
| proper / common | fragment | **prepositional** | **dependent** |
| singular / plural | **subject** | **appositive** | structure |
| **pronoun** | **predicate** | **verbal** | simple |
| subject / object | simple / complete | gerund | compound |
| relative | **direct object** | participle | complex |
| demonstrative | **indirect object** | infinitive | compound-complex |
| person, 1, 2, 3 | **subject complement** | | purpose |
| **adjective** | predicate nom | | declarative |
| degree | predicate adj | | imperative |
| article | | | interrogative |
| definite | | | exclamatory |
| indefinite | | | |
| **verb** | | | |
| tense | | | |
| perfect tenses | | | |
| helping verb | | | |
| singular / plural | | | |
| active / passive voice | | | |
| action / linking | | | |
| mood | | | |
| **adverb** | | | |
| **conjunction** | | | |
| coordinating | | | |
| subordinating | | | |
| correlative | | | |
| **preposition** | | | |
| object of prep | | | |
| **interjection** | | | |

# 1

## parts of speech

parts of the sentence

phrases

clauses

## Level One: Eight Parts of Speech

**Parts of speech**: The parts of speech are the eight kinds of words: **noun**, **pronoun**, **adjective**, **verb**, **adverb**, **preposition**, **conjunction**, and **interjection**. Only eight! It is miraculous to have so simple a system for sorting all the words in our huge language. What if we had been assigned the problem of finding how many kinds of words there are in the English language? Would we have discovered a system this easy? Never! We are lucky that—in addition to the eight parts of speech we already have to learn—we do not also have to learn dozens or even hundreds of other parts of speech, such as (just imagine) adnouns, projectives, interverbs, preverbs, postpositions, conjections, disjunctions, and surnouns. From this viewpoint, the eight-category part of speech system is a masterpiece of intelligent simplicity. It is *elegant* in the sense that scientists describe a simple theory as **elegant**.

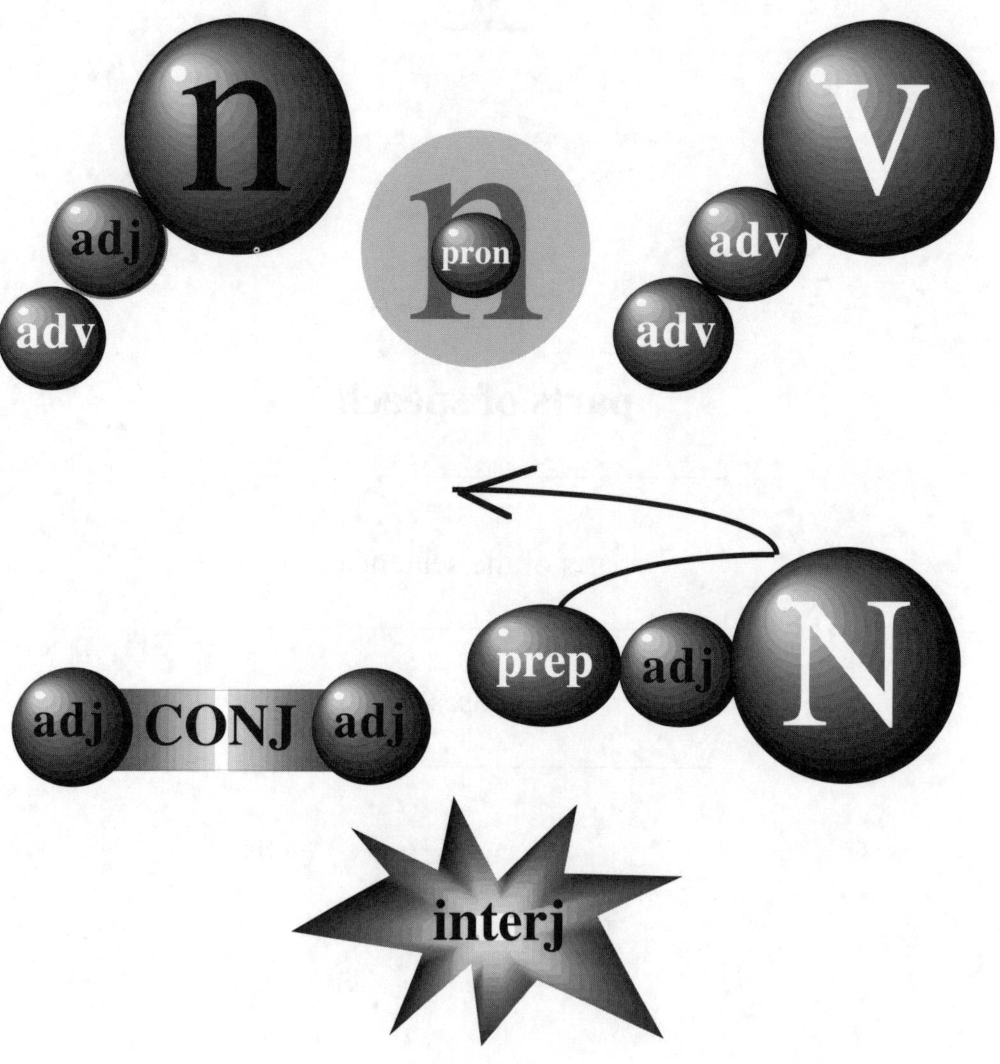


**There are only eight kinds of words!**

# Latin: ***nomen***, name.

## NOUN

**The name of a person, place, or thing.**

**Noun**: (n.) A noun (from Latin *nomen*, name) is the name of a person, place, or thing [*Mozart, Chicago, epidermis, rock, freedom, pulchritude*]. **Proper nouns** (*Mozart*) are capitalized, and **common nouns** (*epidermis*) are not. **Concrete nouns** (*rock*) are names of objects, and **abstract nouns** (*freedom, pulchritude*) are names of ideas. When we call someone by name, the person's name is called the **noun of direct address** (*Livingston*, I presume.). A noun that names a group, such as *flock*, is known as a **collective noun**. Nouns are **singular** (sing.) if they describe individual things, or **plural** (pl.) if they describe multiple things: *boat/boats, flock/flocks, kindness/kindnesses*.

In Walt Whitman's sentence from his great poem *Leaves of Grass*, "O Captain! my captain! rise up and hear the bells," *Captain* is a noun of direct address, and the subject of the verb *rise* is understood to be second person, since the sentence is imperative. In William Shakespeare's *The Taming of the Shrew*, Katherine calls Petruchio "a mad-brain rudesby full of spleen"! Few of us, one imagines, would like to be named by the noun *rudesby*, mad-brained or otherwise.

**Nouns from Robert Louis Stevenson's *Treasure Island***: In his 1881 masterpiece, *Treasure Island*, Robert Louis Stevenson used nouns, especially nautical nouns, such as *forecastle, palisade, doldrums, hummock, miscreant, doubloon, buccaneer, capstan, quay, sward, gunwale, lancet, rogue, bowsprit, hawser, slough*, and *truculence*, to give an exotic sense of adventure and romance to his sea tale. Is there a noun from *Treasure Island* that you don't know?

**A Classic Noun: *Visage***: The noun *visage*, that indicates the face or the expression on the face, is a true classic noun, that has been in literary use for centuries. Chaucer, for example, used *visage* in his immortal *Canterbury Tales*, written in 1385; he wrote that "This olde man gan loke in his visage," and referred to "Many fair shap and many a fair visage." We even see "Of his visage children were aferd." The changes in spelling over the last five centuries are dramatic. Shakespeare used *visage* in *A Midsummer Night's Dream* to describe how Phoebe doth behold *"Her silver visage in the watery glass*." And in *Romeo and Juliet* we read, "Give me a case to put my visage in" referring to a mask! In modern literature, *visage* continues to have an important role; Joseph Heller, in his 1955 *Catch-22*, described "the sheer force of his solemn, domineering visage," and Robert Penn Warren, in his 1946 *All the King's Men* wrote that "Mr. Patton's granite visage seemed to lean toward me like a monument about to fall."

**Four-Level Analysis:** Frequently in *The Magic Lens*, you will see a four-level analysis of a sentence from a famous work of literature. Often, most of the analysis will be in gray, letting focus elements be highlighted in black. Even though we haven't studied some of the levels or terms yet, you will still get a brief preview of them. As we learn more, more of the analysis will make sense. In the four-level analysis below, you can see that at the parts of speech level, *Americans* and *summer* are nouns, while at the parts of sentence level each noun plays a different role. *Americans* is the subject of the sentence, and *summer* is a direct object. We'll learn what a direct object is soon.

## FOUR-LEVEL ANALYSIS

### From Martin Luther King's *Why We Can't Wait:*

| | Americans | awaited | a | quiet | summer. |
|---|---|---|---|---|---|
| **Parts of Speech:** | **noun** | v. | adj. | adj. | **noun** |
| **Parts of Sentence:** | subject | predicate | | | direct object |
| **Phrases:** | | no phrases | | | |
| **Clauses:** | one independent clause, a simple declarative sentence | | | | |

Here we see both a proper noun and a common noun, a plural noun and a singular noun. The proper plural noun is used as the subject of an action verb, and the singular common noun is used as the direct object.

## Nouns from *The Word Within the Word* • List #1

In the sentences below, the words in **bold** contain important Latin or Greek stems. Which of the words in bold are nouns? For each **bold** word that is a noun, put an *n.* in the blank to the right.

1. The Civil War **antedates** the Korean War by decades. ______________
2. The **anti-aircraft** fire shot down the enemy planes. ______________
3. The two nations have a **bilateral** agreement. ______________
4. The **circumspect** spy is difficult to catch. ______________
5. The two together are an interesting **combination.** ______________
6. Stubb was **confined** to the ship's hold. ______________
7. The lunar lander **descended** through the atmosphere. ______________
8. Queequeg's attention was not easily **distracted.** ______________
9. She made an **equilateral** triangle with three straws. ______________
10. It was an **extraordinary** achievement. ______________
11. They were lost in **interstellar** space. ______________
12. He received an **intravenous** solution through a tube in his arm. ______________
13. The boy was a lonely **introvert** who kept to himself. ______________
14. He looked fearfully at the glowing, **malevolent** demon. ______________
15. Ishmael had the **misfortune** to forget his wallet. ______________
16. The Pequod's voyage is not a **nonprofit** endeavor. ______________
17. Flask added a **postscript** at the bottom of the letter. ______________
18. Before Romeo left, Juliet had a frightening **premonition.** ______________
19. The circle was divided into two equal **semicircles.** ______________
20. The lieutenant gave a sharp order to her **subordinate.** ______________

**PRONOUN**

**A word that takes the place of a noun.**

**Pronoun**: (pron.) Pronouns refer. They refer to nouns. A pronoun is a word that we use instead of repeating an **antecedent** (noun); this helps us avoid repeating the antecedent (*ante*: before, *cede*: go) noun over again monotonously. For example, we don't say "Hamlet went to New York where Hamlet went to the opera." How tedious! Instead, we replace the second *Hamlet* with a pronoun: "Hamlet went to New York where *he* went to the opera." By avoiding monotonous repetition of lengthy or compound nouns, *pronouns make language fast*.

Pronouns may be **masculine gender** (*he, him, his*), **feminine gender** (*she, her, hers*) or **neuter gender** (*it*). Pronouns may also have **person** and **number**:

| **Subject Pronouns** | **Singular** | **Plural** |
|---|---|---|
| **First person:** | I | we |
| **Second person:** | you | you |
| **Third person:** | he, she, it | they |

**Antecedent**: The pronoun's antecedent is the noun the pronoun replaces. The antecedent is named for the fact that it goes (cede) before (ante) its pronoun, and the pronoun refers back to—or replaces—the antecedent. **Hamlet** was he.

**There isn't always an antecedent.** Though understanding the concept of the antecedent is essential to learning pronouns, it must be said that some pronouns do not operate as antecedent replacers. The indefinite pronouns, for example, do not operate as simple antecedent replacers: **Anyone** who is registered may vote.

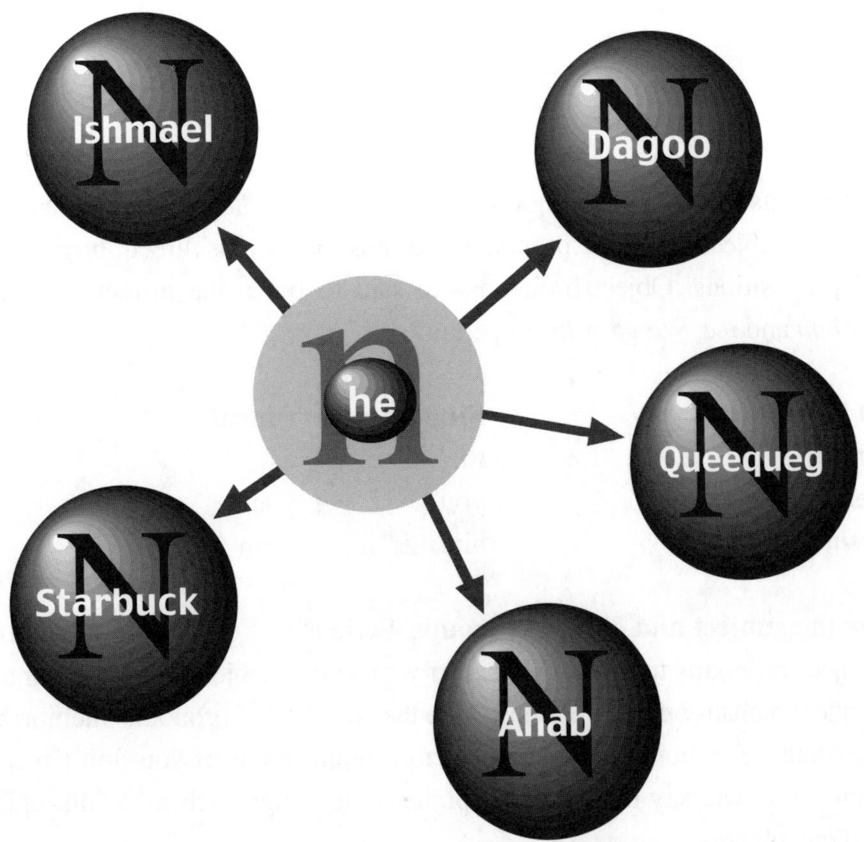


**Pronoun non-specificity**: Pronouns are NOT specific! They are general. The pronoun *he* refers equally to all male organisms in the world! This ambiguity causes problems when we try to force pronouns—against their universal nature—to stick to a single reference. If you write *he* in a sentence, *he* will attempt to refer to all males mentioned in your paragraph, or even to all males mentioned in your page.

**Caution**: If you need review on the parts of the sentence (the various kinds of subjects and objects), you may wish to skip ahead to review or preview the parts of the sentence.

## It is I, Hamlet the Dane!

**Subject pronouns**: The subject pronouns are *I*, *you*, *he*, *she*, *it*, *we*, *you*, and *they*, and they are just what their name suggests: we use them to make subjects. They may be used as *subjects* of clauses and as *subject* complements. They are not to be used as objects. Subject pronouns are said to be in the **subject case**. The subject case is also called the **nominative** case. Examples: *It* was *I*. *She* and *I* went to the cathedral. From Shakespeare: "It is *I*, Hamlet, the Dane!" From Whitman: "I am *he* who aches of amorous love."

| **Subject Pronouns** | **Singular** | **Plural** |
|---|---|---|
| **1st Person** | I | we |
| **2nd Person** | you | you |
| **3d Person** | he, she, it | they |

**Object pronouns**: The object pronouns are *me*, *you*, *him*, *her*, *it*, *us*, *you*, and *them*, and they are pronouns used as objects: they are pronouns that must be used as direct *objects*, indirect *objects*, and *objects* of prepositions. Object pronouns are said to be in the **object case**. It hit *me*. The present was for *him* and *me*. We gave *him* a petunia.

| **Object Pronouns** | **Singular** | **Plural** |
|---|---|---|
| **1st Person** | me | us |
| **2nd Person** | you | you |
| **3d Person** | him, her, it | them |

**Memorize the subject and object pronouns.** Seriously. You *have* to memorize them. Since we use only subject pronouns for all subjects, and we use only object pronouns for all objects, and since it is a blunder to misuse them, you must have the two lists of pronouns memorized (and know the parts of the sentence) if you are ever to master pronoun usage. If you don't memorize the two cases of pronouns, you will say odious and reprehensible things such as, "This epistle is for you and I." You and *me*, please.

He saw he?

Him saw him?

Him saw he?

**He** saw **him.**

**Thompson's Pronoun rule: A subject is a subject and an object is an object**. In other words, use subject pronouns as subjects of clauses and as subject complements; use object pronouns as direct objects, indirect objects, and objects of prepositions. *It* was *he*, but *they* saw *him*. The accolade was for *him* and *me*. (This explanation will make more sense later after we have studied parts of the sentence; at that time, come back and look at this section again, and combine the two discussions together in your mind.)

# A **subject** is a **subject**, and an **object** is an **object.**

**In other words,** any part of the sentence called a **subject** (subject of clause or subject complement) uses a subject pronoun. Any part of sentence called an **object** (direct object, indirect object, or object of preposition) uses an object pronoun. **A subject is a subject, and an object is an object**. If you know the subject and object pronouns, and you know the parts of the sentence, then pronoun usage is *easy*: just use a subject pronoun for any sentence subject, and use an object pronoun for any sentence object. If you don't know your pronouns and sentence parts, pronoun usage is impossible!

| **Subject Pronouns**<br>(Pronouns for Subjects) | **Object Pronouns**<br>(Pronouns for Objects) |
|---|---|
| **I** | **me** |
| **you** | **you** |
| **he she it** | **him her it** |
| **we** | **us** |
| **you** | **you** |
| **they** | **them** |

## FOUR-LEVEL ANALYSIS

**From Walt Whitman's *Leaves of Grass:***

| | **I** | **am** | **he** | **who** | **aches** | **of** | **amorous** | **love.** |
|---|---|---|---|---|---|---|---|---|
| **Parts of Speech:** | **subj. pron.** | v. | **subj. pron.** | **pron.** | v. | prep. | adj. | **noun** |
| **Parts of Sentence:** | subject | predicate | subject complement | | | | direct object | |
| **Phrases:** | | | | | | -----prepositional phrase----- | | |
| **Clauses:** | ----independent clause---- | | --------------------dependent clause-------------------- | | | | | |
| | two clause, a complex declarative sentence | | | | | | | |

In Whitman's sentence, he uses a subject pronoun, *I*, for the subject of the verb and also for the subject complement (*he*). We will study these parts of sentence later, but for now, just notice that we change pronoun case to match the part of sentence. Whitman also uses the relative pronoun, *who*, to begin his adjective clause.

**The song of the subjects, and the song of the objects**: Sometimes, we refer to other languages as singsong, and yet, English also has its musical qualities. We do not normally hear the musical qualities of English, because it is so familiar, but when we listen closely, the songs are there. One of the most important is the difference between the sound of subject pronouns and the sound of object pronouns, a sound that lets us keep our ideas clear, even in spontaneous speech. If the subjects of sentences *sound* different, it makes it easy to spot them when words are coming rapidly.

I he she we they

**eye-eee-ayay-eye-eee**

me him her us them

**mmm-urrr-uhh-mmm**

**Possessive pronouns**: A possessive pronoun is a pronoun that shows possession (I realize that this comes as a shock!) and that is used as both a pronoun and as an adjective in order to indicate ownership or possession. Possessive pronouns include: *my*, *your*, *his*, *her*, *its*, *our*, and *their*. The possessive case pronouns are *already possessive, and therefore do not need apostrophes*. Diego lost *his* pesos. The dog found *its* doghouse.

# My noun!

**Its or it's?** The word *its* is a possessive pronoun. The word *it's* is a contraction of *it* and *is*. The apostrophe replaces the missing *i*. *It's* too late to lock *its* cage. Do not, not, not use the possessive apostrophe in the possessive pronoun.

**it’is**

**Interrogative pronouns**: An interrogative pronoun is just what its name suggests: it's a pronoun used to interrogate: *who, whose, whom, which, what. Who* went to the piazza?

**Demonstrative pronouns:** A demonstrative pronoun is a pronoun used to demonstrate: *this, that, these, those. This* is the dog I wish you to paint. *That* is the opinion of a Philistine.

**Demonstrative pronouns as subjects:** It is a good idea not to use demonstrative pronouns as subjects, because they have a tendency to be vague or ambiguous. For example, it is better to write, "*This theory of gravitation influenced people*," than "*This influenced people*."

**Relative pronouns:** A relative pronoun is a pronoun that relates an adjective clause to a main clause. The relative pronouns often begin short adjective clauses that interrupt main clauses. The man *who followed you* turned left. The relative pronouns are *who, whose, whom , which, that.*

***Who* or *whom*?** *Who* is a subject, and *whom* is an object. The composer *who* wrote the *Brandenburg Concerto* was Bach. You asked *whom*?

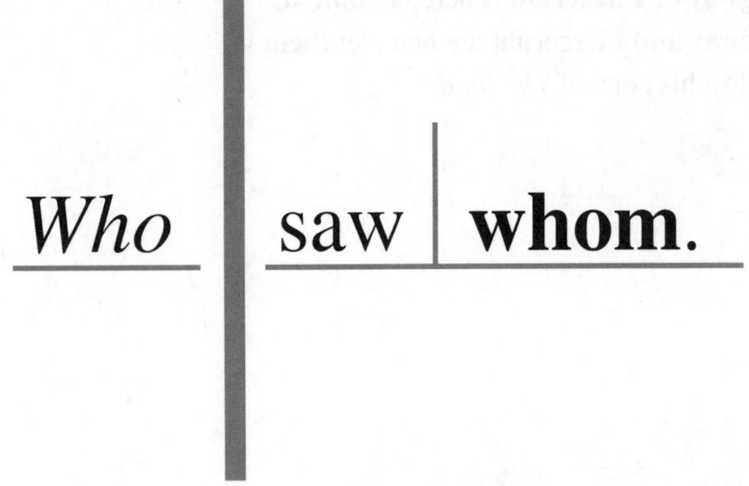

**Reflexive pronouns**: A reflexive pronoun is a -self or -selves pronoun that reflects back to a word used previously in the sentence. I found *myself* awash on a strange beach.

**Indefinite**: The indefinite pronouns are general pronouns that do not have definite antecedents: *anyone, anybody, each, all.* Those ending in -one and -body are singular.

**Intensive pronouns**: An intensive pronoun is a -self or -selves pronoun that is used to intensify the emphasis on a noun or another pronoun. I *myself* agree with that idea.

**Types of Pronouns**

**Subject**: *I, you, he, she, it, we, you, they*
**Object**: *me, you, him, her, it, us, you, them*
**Possessive**: *my, your, his, her, its, our their*
**Interrogative**: *who, whose, whom, which, what*
**Demonstrative**: *this, that, these, those*
**Relative**: *who, whose, whom, which, that*
**Indefinite**: *anyone, anybody, each, all,* etc.
**Reflexive**: *myself, yourself, himsel*f, etc.
**Intensive**: *myself, yourself, himself,* etc.

# Can we agree?

**Pronoun/antecedent agreement in number**: A pronoun must agree with its antecedent in number. If the noun is singular, the pronoun must be singular also.

**Alexander** brought the column to a halt; **he** summoned his mapmaker.
The **soldiers** found Archimedes; **they** did not recognize the crazy old man.
**Crick and Watson** discovered the double helix; **they** won the Nobel Prize.
If **Hemingway or Fitzgerald** is here, let **him** in.
If **Hemingway and Fitzgerald** are here, let **them** in.
**Someone** lost **his** copy of *The Iliad*.

**Pronoun reference problems**: One of the most common problems new writers have with grammar is the **pronoun reference error** (ref). As a result of their universal nature, pronouns are so problem-prone that they almost seem to be malicious, deliberately causing confusion wherever they can. The crux of the problem lies in pronouns not doing what we intend them to do: we intend them to refer to and only to their antecedents. In other words, a pronoun is supposed to stand for a noun. We say *he* instead of saying *Hamlet*, or we say *it* instead of saying *the committee*. As long as it is clear what noun the pronoun replaces, everything is fine. But what if the replacement is not clear? What if we say, *Crick and Watson went to the beach, where he broke his foot.* Well, who broke whose foot?

**Everyone is singular!** Remember that the *-one* and *-body* indefinite pronouns are all singular, even though they may not seem to be when you first consider them. Some singular pronouns: *someone*, *somebody*, *everyone*, *everybody*, *each*, *every*. Someone lost **his** pliers. (Not **their** pliers, someone is not they.)

**His, or her, or his or her?** In order to avoid the **number disagreement** in a sentence such as *Someone dropped* **their** muffler, we used to select the masculine gender pronoun *his*: *Someone dropped* **his** muffler. We might call this the **macho solution.** While the macho solution correctly avoided the number disagreement, it also created a new problem: it tended to ground our language in a male viewpoint, a bias that modern egalitarian political philosophies correctly deplore. One popular solution to this problem of masculine bias is the **compound gender solution**: *Someone dropped* **his or her** muffler. This solution avoids the number disagreement, and offers political balance, and yet to some ears the compound gender solution sounds awkward. Perhaps the most graceful solution is to use the right gender pronoun when possible (Darius rode his chariot) and otherwise to use an article rather than a pronoun if the gender pronoun is not appropriate. We might call this solution the **article escape**: *Someone dropped* **a** muffler.

Some of the common pronoun reference errors are:

The **missing antecedent**, in which there is no antecedent noun to which the pronoun could possibly refer. (Example: beginning the first paragraph of a term paper with "*He* was born in 1895." He who?)

The **ambiguous reference**, in which there are two or more possible nouns to which the pronoun might refer. (Dickens hastened to meet his editor, but *he* was late. Who was late, Dickens or the editor?)

# Some**one** is not they!

The **adolescent they** error (Roy Copperud's term), in which we use *they* or *their* to refer to a singular antecedent (If someone wants a burger, *they* have to buy one). We assume that in describing number disagreement this way, Copperud intended to indicate that number disagreement is a problem that especially bedevils young writers and speakers. The truth is that adults make this mistake too; in fact, John Stuart Mill used the adolescent they in his brilliant essay.

John Stuart Mill's adolescent they:

"If either a public officer or anyone else saw a person attempting to cross a bridge which had been ascertained to be unsafe, and there were no time to warn him of his danger, they might seize him and turn him back."
-On Liberty

## **This** is vague...

The **ghost demonstration** error, in which we use the demonstrative pronoun *this* as a subject of a clause, assuming incorrectly that the reader is sure what *this* refers to. The ghost demonstration error could cause vagueness or ambiguity, or could be based on a missing antecedent. *This* soon resulted in . . . This what?

**Solutions to pronoun reference errors**: Usually, the best solution is to replace the problem pronouns with nouns. Otherwise, think and rewrite.

## FOUR-LEVEL ANALYSIS

### From Mary Shelley's *Frankenstein:*

| | He | appeared | to despise | himself. |
|---|---|---|---|---|
| **Parts of Speech:** | **subject pronoun** | v. | adv. | **reflexive pronoun** |
| **Parts of Sentence:** | subject | predicate | | |
| **Phrases:** | | | --------infinitive phrase----------- | |
| **Clauses:** | one independent clause, a simple declarative sentence | | | |

Mary Shelley has used a third person singular masculine gender pronoun as the subject of her idea, and also worked in a nice reflexive pronoun that reflects back upon the subject. Notice that *to despise* is treated as one word; that is how we will treat infinitives (explanation later!)

## Pronouns from *The Word Within the Word* • List #2

In the sentences below, the words in **bold** contain important Latin or Greek stems. Many of the sentences also contain pronouns, though they are not in **bold**. Underline each pronoun you see, and in the blank at the right, write in the type of pronoun it is: subject, object, demonstrative, etc.

1. It is, or once was, ruled by a **monarchy.** ________________
2. The **dullard** was always boring everyone to tears. ________________
3. In killing his father, Oedipus was guilty of **patricide**. ________________
4. She is an electronic **technician**. ________________
5. The **dermatitis** on his skin was painful and unpleasant. ________________
6. Balthazar, the scuba diver, collects them—**aquatic** species. ________________
7. The deaf moose had injured his **auditory** nerve. ________________
8. **Belligerent** nations gain nothing from their many wars. ________________
9. The hostile island tribe **captured** them. ________________
10. He **incised** the design into the oaken door with a knife. ________________
11. **Biomorphic** abstract sculpture resembles these. ________________
12. Patton wrote a tedious **autobiography** about his exploits. ________________
13. The **porter** will carry your bags to the train. ________________
14. Please **inscribe** my yearbook. ________________
15. Since Ishmael loved insects, he studied **entomology**. ________________
16. The grand jury returned a robbery **indictment** against him. ________________
17. A **credulous** person will believe that. ________________
18. Fortunately, the **centipede** wears its shoes. ________________
19. Ishmael was a **neophyte** in whaling, but he learned quickly. ________________
20. He, Ahab, was a lifelong **bibliophile**. ________________

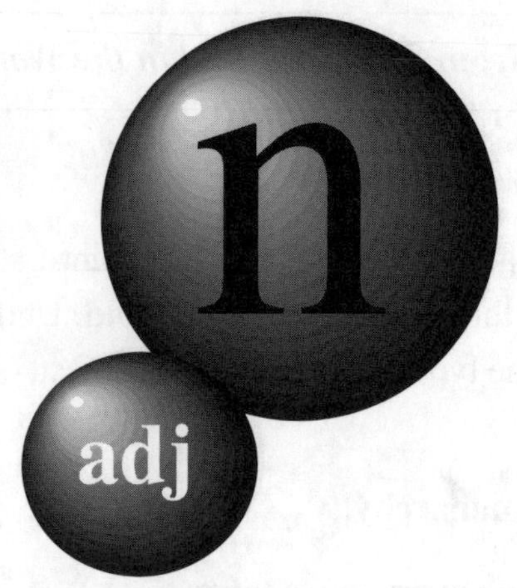


## ADJECTIVE

**A word that modifies a noun or pronoun.**

**Adjective**: (adj.) An adjective is a word that modifies a noun or a pronoun: the *red* car. An adjective can be used as a subject complement: The swim was *good*. Why would we wish to modify a noun or pronoun? Instead of modifying nouns with adjectives, why not just use a better noun? Wouldn't it be better to use nouns all the time, and avoid adjectives? Well, even if it were desirable, it would be impossible, because we have only thousands of nouns, but there are billions of things in the universe. We need adjectives to help us describe things for which no exact nouns exist, and to describe all of the things for which we do not know the exact noun. Adjectives also help us to express the subtle differences between very similar things.

**Modify?** To modify is to change. In what way do adjectives modify nouns? Imagine a **frozen** summit. Think about the frozen summit of the mountain until you can see it in your mind. Now, imagine a **political** summit. Does the second adjective modify (change) the image that you have in your mind?

# Adjectives **modify** the nouns of the mind.

For example, the adjectives in a novel modify the images we imagine as we read the novel. Some definitions say that an adjective *describes* a noun, but *modify* is better because nouns truly are modified or changed by their adjectives.

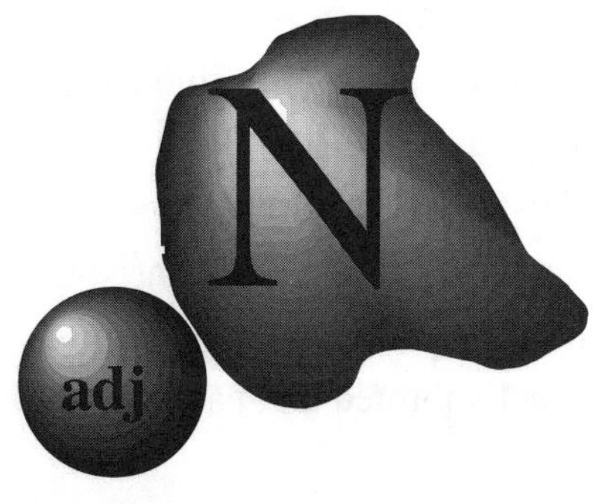


**Binary**: Notice that an adjective is always part of a binary system, like a double star or a planet with one moon. The presence of an adjective implies the presence of a noun or pronoun. Every modifier modifies a modified. If you see *the* in a sentence, look for the noun. A noun can do without an adjective, but an adjective can not exist without a noun or pronoun. If it isn't modifying a noun or pronoun, it *isn't* an adjective. So we can say that an adjective modifies *its* noun, because there is a belonging, a connectedness.

**Three degrees of adjectives**: Adjectives have a wonderful property: they can change degree. A fire can be hot, hotter, or hottest. Ice can be cold, colder, or coldest. A book can be good, better, or best. These three **degrees** of adjective intensity are known as the **positive** (*good*), **comparative** (*better*), and **superlative** (*best*) degrees. These degrees allow us to make clear comparisons between similar nouns.

| good | **better** | ***best*** |
|---|---|---|
| positive | comparative | superlative |

**Proper adjectives**: Proper adjectives are made out of proper nouns. *England* makes *English. Rome* makes *Roman.* When we convert the proper noun *Spain* into the proper adjective *Spanish*, we retain the capitalization. In south Florida, Spanish moss hangs from the trees. The reason a school subject such as English or Spanish is capitalized and a subject such as history or mathematics is not is that *English* and *Spanish* are proper adjectives made from the proper names of countries.

Spain
Spanish

**Articles**: The articles are the three adjectives *a*, *an*, and *the*. The **definite article** is *the*, and the **indefinite articles** are *a* and *an*. Notice how logical these names are: we are being **definite** when we ask for *the* book, but we are being **indefinite** when we ask for *a* book. The word *article* comes from the Latin word *artus*, meaning "joint." Where's the joint? Well, imagine if we had no *the*, *a*, or *an*; in rapid speech sounds would blur together, and we might not be able to tell where the nouns were! The articles are little noun-alerts, that sound little bleeps right before nouns, letting us know that what comes next is probably a noun. These little articles break the sentence into nouny segments, like an insect's jointed leg, each segment beginning with a noun alert!

**The** galleon reached **the** port quickly, without **a** mishap, sailing silently past **the** towering fort, with **the** lights of **the** city making **a** glistening path over **the** water.

**Español:** In Spanish, there are masculine and feminine articles! Every noun is either masculine or feminine, and is designated by a masculine definite article, ***el***, or a feminine definite article, ***la***. So whereas in English we simply say ***the*** book or ***the*** window, the books in Spanish we have to change gender between *el libro* and *la ventana*. The articles also change to agree with nouns' singular and plural number:

| | |
|---|---|
| **the** book | **el** libro |
| **the** books | **los** libro**s** |
| **the** window | **la** ventan**a** |
| **the** windows | **las** ventan**as** |

Imagine that the English definite article and nouns behaved as the Spanish ones do. What if all English nouns had gender, with the masculine nouns ending in -o and the feminine nouns ending in -a, and we also changed the articles to something like:

the booko
thes bookos
tha windowa
thas windowas

The feeling of Spanish gender-grammar is poetic, as though all things are alive, animate, rather than being inanimate neutral objects. The English definite article *the* expresses part of an anthropocentric world view that regards humankind as primary, other species as practically inanimate, and other phenomena as "inanimate objects." This material view of reality can be detected in the unisex English article.

**Good or well?** The word *good* is an adjective that may be used to modify nouns or pronouns; the word *well* is usually an adverb that modifies verbs, adjectives, or other adverbs. The *good* athlete runs *well*. We should not say, "I don't feel well," which means that one has no talent for feeling things! We should say, "I don't feel good," which uses the adjective *good* to modify the pronoun *I*.

**Adjectives from James M. Barrie's *Peter Pan*:** In *Peter Pan*, which he wrote in 1904, James M. Barrie used adjectives such as *rakish, tedious, delectable, unwonted, deft, placid, amiable, elegant, tremulous, debonair, genial, cadaverous, profound, amorous, indomitable, plaintive, fastidious, exquisite, succulent, incisive, impassive, sanguinary, vivid, dodgy, sublime, subtle, malignant, phlegmatic, aloof, somber, nether, adept, inscrutable, bacchanalian*, and *strident* to convey the dreamlike, imaginative images of Never Never Land. Which of these adjectives do you not know? Which ones would best describe Peter?

**Adjectives in a sentence from James Hilton's *Lost Horizon*:** Look at these adjectives from Hilton's novel *Lost Horizon*. Hilton is using adjectives heavily, modifying his nouns gracefully. What is your favorite adjective/noun combination in this sentence?

> There was something rather **Elizabethan** about him—his **casual** versatility, his **good** looks, that **effervescent** combination of **mental** with **physical** activities.

**A Classic Adjective, *Serene*:** The adjective *serene* has been an important modifier in English and American literature, giving an important twist to hundreds of nouns. Coming from a Greek word meaning dry, *serene* refers to things that are calm, peaceful, and clear, such as a blue sky. Milton referred to serene angels in *Paradise Lost*, Daniel Defoe described serene weather in *Robinson Crusoe*, and in *Frankenstein*, Mary Shelley's monster observed that "A serene sky and verdant fields filled me with ecstasy." Henry David Thoreau, in *Walden*, noted that his "serenity is rippled but not ruffled." In *Invisible Man*, Ralph Ellison wrote that "he seemed too serene and too far away." In Kenneth Grahame's *The Wind in the Willows*, he describes the moon as "serene and detached in a cloudless sky." Mark Twain once said, "If you see an adjective, kill it." In his classic novel *Tom Sawyer*, however, he described how we "heard the stony-hearted liar reel off his serene statement."

**We heard the "stony-hearted liar reel off his serene statement."**

**From Aldous Huxley's *Brave New World:***

| | **He** | **had** | **a** | **long** | **chin** | **and** | **big,** | **rather** | **prominent** | **teeth.** |
|---|---|---|---|---|---|---|---|---|---|---|
| **Parts of Speech:** | pron | v. | **adj.** | **adj.** | n. | conj. | **adj.** | adv. | **adj.** | n. |
| **Parts of Sentence:** | subject | pred. | ----------------------compound direct object---------------------------------- | | | | | | | |
| **Phrases:** | | | no prepositional, appositive, or verbal phrases | | | | | | | |
| **Clauses:** | | | one independent clause, a simple declarative sentence | | | | | | | |

Huxley's sentence has a cold objectivity that is brought to the sentence by the adjectives. Notice how innocuous the sentence is if we leave out the modifiers: He had a chin and teeth! Adjectives can transform a sentence.

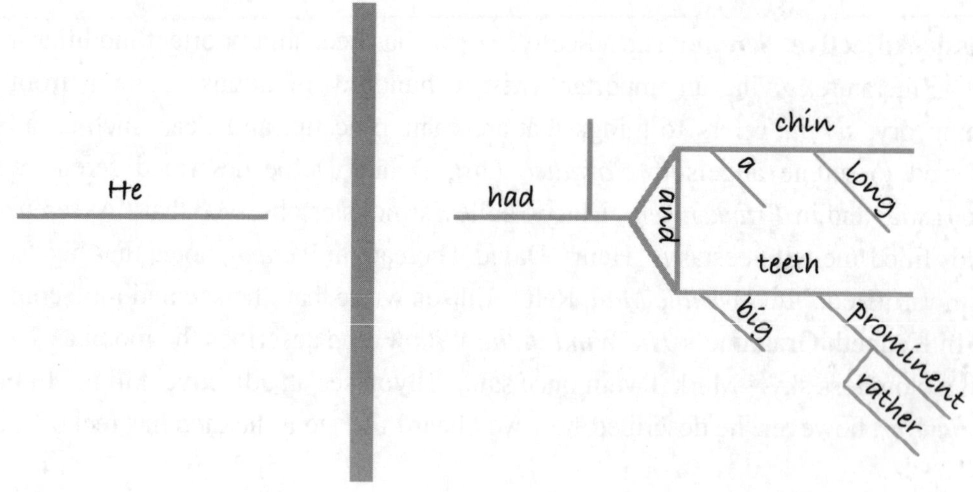

## Adjectives from *The Word Within the Word* • List #3

In the sentences below, the words in **bold** contain important Latin or Greek stems. The words in *italics*, including those in both bold and italics, are the subject of this exercise. For each word in italics, write either *noun* or *adjective* in the blank at the right.

1. English contains *many* **homophones** like two and too. __________
2. It was a ***specious*** argument, but it sounded convincing. __________
3. The *callow* youth was **inducted** into the army. __________
4. The **transfer** was made in the darkness of a *moonless* night. __________
5. The patent is still **pending** on the secret *product*. __________
6. The *two* bacteria were only a **micron** apart. __________
7. The fire **hydrant** stood in *front* of the school. __________
8. An overexposure to *the* sun's **photons** gave her a sunburn. __________
9. The swift god Apollo was a member of the *Greek* **pantheon**. __________
10. He wore a **pentagram** on his sleeve, not an *ordinary* pentagon. __________
11. The strange boy could move distant objects by ***telekinesis***. __________
12. The wild creature had an ***omnivorous*** appetite. __________
13. The surgeon was able to **excise** the *malignant* tissue. __________
14. Johann Sebastian Bach composed ***polyphonic*** music. __________
15. The crash victims suffered ***hypothermia*** on the frozen tundra. __________
16. The amoeba uses its *flowing* **pseudopods** to move. __________
17. The human brain is said to contain over 100 *billion* **neurons**. __________
18. Iron ore is called ***hematite*** because of its red color. __________
19. *Single-celled* animals are known as the **Protozoa**. __________
20. Laws against ***vivisection*** prevent cruelty to animals. __________

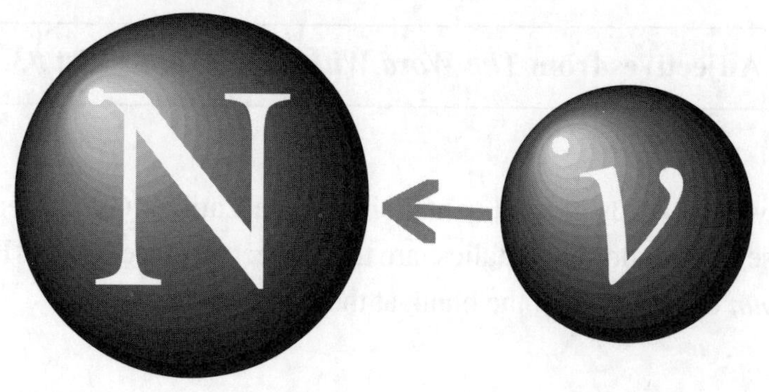


**The verb is**
**about**
**the noun.**

**VERB**

**A word that shows action, being, or links a subject to a subject complement.**

**Verb**: (v.) A verb is a word that shows action, or being, or links a subject to a subject complement. The verb tells what the noun does or is. If the verb is an action verb, then it might show action on a direct object: *Verdi composed the opera*. Or, an action verb might show simple action not on a direct object: *Verdi composed.* If the verb is linking, then it might link the subject to a subject complement: He *is*. He *is* a poet. Most verbs show actions or make equations.

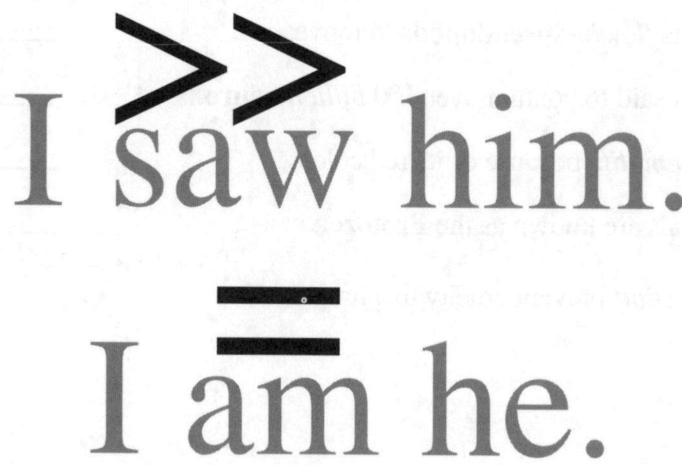

**The verb is about the noun**. Every sentence has a subject, and the verb (the predicate of the sentence) is about it. The subject will always be a noun or subject pronoun, and the simple predicate is the verb. This means that the verb is about the noun. The verb is saying that the noun did something or that the noun is something.

**Four principal parts of the verb:** All verb forms are made out of four primary forms that each verb possesses. These four primary forms are called the verb's **principal parts**. The four principal parts are:

the **infinitive**: to do (do), to go (go), to think (think), to dream (dream)
the **present participle**: doing, going, thinking, dreaming, ascending
the **past**: did, went, thought, dreamed
the **past participle**: done, gone, thought, dreamed

**Regular verbs**: Most verbs make the four principle parts in the same regular way, and therefore, we refer to these ordinary verbs as **regular verbs.** These regular verbs always begin with the infinitive, add **-ing** to make the present participle, and add **-d** or **-ed** to make the past and past participle:

| infinitive | present participle | past | past participle |
|---|---|---|---|
| to work | working | worked | worked |
| to spill | spilling | spilled | spilled |

**Irregular verbs**: Many verbs do not follow this regular pattern. Instead, they have principal parts that are unique and that must therefore be memorized in order to be used correctly:

to shrink, shrinking, shrank, shrunk
to ring, ringing, rang, rung
to break, breaking, broke, broken
to write, writing, wrote, written

**Auxiliary or helping verbs**: In a **simple tense** the verb stands alone, as a single word, to make the simple predicate. In a **compound tense**, the main verb is supplemented by an **auxiliary** or **helping** verb to construct the tense. The future and prefect tenses are examples of compound tenses that use auxiliary verbs. In the sentence *I will have composed a symphony* the main verb is *composed* and the auxiliary verbs are *will have*.

**Transitive verb:** (v.t.) A transitive verb is an action verb that acts on a direct object: The harpoon *hit* Moby Dick.

**Intransitive verb:** (v.i.) An intransitive verb is an action verb that does not act on a direct object: Harpoons *flew*."

**Why we call them "transitive"**: Transitive verbs are action verbs that are called *transitive* because of the **transit** of action or energy that takes place when the subject acts on the object. If I kick the bucket, the energy **trans**fers from me to the bucket I am kicking. The stem *trans* means "across." In an intransitive verb, there is no transfer of energy.

**trans**

**transfer**

**transAmerican**

**transcontinental**

**transit**

**transitive**

**Active voice verb:** An active voice verb is an action verb that shows the subject acting. Active voice is usually more vigorous than passive voice. "Johnson *discussed* the problem" is active voice.

**Passive voice verb:** A passive voice verb is an action verb that shows the subject passively being acted upon: The problem *was discussed*. Passive voice can make sentences seem weak, since the subject of the sentence is not doing anything, and passive voice also tends to leave out important information: If I say *The problem was discussed*, we do not know who discussed the problem, but if I say *Johnson and Boswell discussed the problem*, then we have both energy and information. Active voice is vigorous.

**Active voice**: The meteor **struck** the ship.

**Passive voice**: The ship **was struck** by the meteor.

**Active voice**: The Literary Society **presented** Dickens the award.

**Passive voice**: Dickens **was presented** with an award.

**Use of passive voice in scientific writing:** Writers of scientific papers often prefer passive voice and past tense in order to describe the results of experiments and scientific investigations. Rather than write, "First, I administered the placebo," a scientist would write, "Placebos were administered to the control group each morning." In science the impersonality we normally avoid in other fields makes sense because it contributes to the inductive, objective, and descriptive tone of scientific inquiry. In writing papers on literary matters and on historical figures, you should avoid passive voice.

## **Action** Verbs can be

**Transitive** or **Intransitive**

**Active** Voice or **Passive** Voice

(Linking verbs are neither!)

# Time makes verbs tense.

**Verb tense**: In *The Great Gatsby*, Scott Fitzgerald wrote, "So we beat on, boats against the current, borne back ceaselessly into the past." True, and we can tell it by the verbs. Verbs show us the poignant temporality of human existence. As living beings, we exist in a moving continuum of time, borne along always, awake or asleep; unable to halt, to slow down, or to return. Time is so central in our experience that we identify it in every sentence we make, and we do it by putting each verb in a time **tense**. In other words, tense gives sentences time. We use six different tenses to indicate time. The six tenses include the three ordinary tenses, and the three perfect tenses:

**Six Verb Tenses**

1. **Present**
2. **Past**
3. **Future**
4. **Present perfect**
5. **Past perfect**
6. **Future Perfect**

In **conjugating** these six verb tenses, we see that verbs, like pronouns, have person (first, second, or third) and number (singular or plural):

| | **present tense** | |
|---|---|---|
| | **singular** | **plural** |
| **First person:** | I protest | We protest |
| **Second person**: | You protest | You protest |
| **Third person:** | He, she, it protests | They protest |

| | **past tense** | |
|---|---|---|
| | **singular** | **plural** |
| **First person:** | I protested | We protested |
| **Second person:** | You protested | You protested |
| **Third person:** | He, she, it protested | They protested |

| | **future tense** | |
|---|---|---|
| | **singular** | **plural** |
| **First person:** | I will (shall) protest | We will (shall) protest |
| **Second person:** | You will protest | You will protest |
| **Third person:** | He, she, it will protest | They will protest |

| | **present perfect tense** | |
|---|---|---|
| | **singular** | **plural** |
| **First person:** | I have protested | We have protested |
| **Second person:** | You have protested | You have protested |
| **Third person:** | He, she, it has protested | They have protested |

| | **past perfect tense** | |
|---|---|---|
| | **singular** | **plural** |
| **First person:** | I had protested | We had protested |
| **Second person:** | You had protested | You had protested |
| **Third person:** | He, she, it had protested | They had protested |

| | **future perfect tense** | |
|---|---|---|
| | **singular** | **plural** |
| **First person:** | I will (shall) have protested | We will have protested |
| **Second person:** | You will have protested | You will have protested |
| **Third person:** | He, she, it will have protested | They will have protested |

## The perfect tenses **have finished**.

**Why we call them** *perfect* tenses: The three perfect tenses are called *perfect* because the word *perfect* comes from the Latin *perficere*, meaning "to finish." The perfect tenses are the tenses of things that are finished, either finished in the past, finished in the present, or finished in the future. Present perfect indicates action that is finished now. When George MacArthur fulfilled his pledge ("I shall return.") to the people of the Phillipines, he said: *I have returned.* Past perfect indicates action that was finished then: *I had returned.* Future perfect indicates action that will be finished in the future: *I shall have returned.*

The word *perficere* further breaks down into the two Latin stems *per* (through) and *fac* (make): the lovely idea is that we are finished with something only when it is perfect, then we are through making it. Notice that the three perfect tenses are the "have" tenses: they all make use of the verb *to have* as a helping verb.

**Progressive forms of the six tenses:** Every one of the six tenses can also be used in a progressive form, an **-ing variation**, indicating action still in progress. First person singular examples of the six tenses' progressive forms:

**Present progressive**: I am protesting.
**Past progressive**: I was protesting.
**Future progressive**: I shall be protesting.
**Present perfect progressive**: I have been protesting.
**Past perfect progressive**: I had been protesting.
**Future perfect progressive**: I shall have been protesting.

**Mood:** In addition to the six verb tenses and the progressive forms of those six tenses, verbs have **mood**. There are three moods: the **indicative**, the **imperative**, and the **subjunctive**. The indicative and imperative moods are not difficult; they are the ordinary forms that we already know. The subjunctive mood, however, is different. We use the subjunctive in IF situations, with the verb *were*. We might say that:

**the indicative is the ordinary mood;**
**the imperative is the command mood, and**
**the subjunctive is the IF mood.**

Examples of the three moods:

**Indicative**: I *am* he.
**Imperative**. *Be* he.
**Subjunctive**: If I *were* he…

**Español and the soft subjunctive:** In English we use the subjunctive mood less frequently than the indicative or imperative moods, but in Spanish the subjunctive is more important. The Spanish subjunctive mood is used to civilize what we say to others, to soften suggestions, to blunt the sharpness of commands, to provide privacy for emotional expressions, and to add gentleness to hopes for things that aren't. It is a way of avoiding the directness of the indicative mood. When expressing a plain statement of fact, the Spanish speaker will indicate the fact with the indicative, but when expressing these more human experiences, the Spanish speaker will shift into the softness of the subjunctive.

| | | |
|---|---|---|
| Indicative | I have a book. | ***Tengo*** un libro |
| Subjunctive | I hope I have a friend. | Espero que ***tenga*** un amigo. |

**Parallel verb tense:** The proofreader's mark for parallel construction is //. Parallelism in tense means sticking to the tense you are using, unless there is a reason to change. Keeping verb tenses parallel is good writing technique. I *went* home, *picked* up the apple, *threw* it through the window, and *laughed*. (all past tense) Don't let your tenses wander; control them. Notice how disturbing the unparallel tenses are in the first passage that follows, and how satisfying the parallel (//) tenses are in the second passage:

**NOT //**

When Charles Dickens **went** to America, he **gives** many speeches, and **feels** that his trip **was** successful. After he **returned** to England, he **begins** to lose the buoyant spirit he **finds** in America, and he **will descend** into melancholy.

**//**

When Charles Dickens **went** to America, he **gave** many speeches, and **felt** that his trip **was** successful. After he **returned** to England, he **began** to lose the buoyant spirit he **found** in America, and he **descended** into melancholy.

**Keep parts of speech parallel in lists and compounds:** Parallel construction (//) also means using uniform parts of speech for items in lists and compounds. Keeping lists and compounds grammatically parallel is a good writing technique. Parallel Compound: *John was adjective and adjective* (John was tall and handsome) is better than *John was adjective and a noun* (John was tall and an athlete). Parallel List: *I want noun, noun, and noun* (I want shelter, clothes and food) is better than *I want noun, noun, and infinitive*. (I want shelter, clothes, and to eat).

**Verbs in Shakespeare's *Romeo and Juliet*:** In the beautiful *Romeo and Juliet*, William Shakespeare used strong verbs to propel the story forward. In *Romeo and Juliet* we see verbs such as *importune*, *retort*, *beseech*, *dissemble*, *disparage*, *impute*, *oppress*, *descry*, *prate*, *feign*, *confound*, *conjure*, *peruse*, *intercede*, *denote*, *doff*, *wax*, *presage*, *impeach*, *inundate*, *abate*, and *vex*—a rich collection of vigorous and human verbs that bring life and emotion to the story. Which verb, more than any other in this list, makes you think of Juliet? Are there any verbs here that you don't know?

**A Classic Verb: *Condescend*:** The verb *condescend* means to stoop down to, to act as though you are superior to someone, and that you have to come down to their low level. *Condescend* was used by Chaucer in 1385, by Milton in 1667, and by Jonathan Swift in 1726. In her 1813 classic *Pride and Prejudice*, Jane Austen wrote, "She had even condescended to advise him to marry as soon as he could." In *Ivanhoe*, written in 1820, Sir Walter Scott's characters are "condescending to avail themselves of the good cheer." In the 1800s, condescend was used by William Thackeray, Emily Bronte, Herman Melville, Charles Dickens, George Eliot, and Thomas Hardy. In his 1901 novel *Kim*, Rudyard Kipling wrote that "she did not condescend to look at them." And in 1911 Frances Hodgson Burnette wrote, in *The Secret Garden*, that "Colin frowned and condescended to look at her."

# ~~didn't~~ did not

# ~~wasn't~~ was not

**Avoid contractions in formal writing.** Lots of verbs are combined with other parts of speech into contractions. A **contraction** is the combination of two or more parts of speech into one word, such as **don't**, **they're**, and **it's**. There is nothing incorrect about the grammar of a contraction, but the contraction is not in keeping with the serious intellectual tone of a formal essay. Contractions suggest that one is in a hurry and doesn't wish to write out each word. Of course, if there are contractions in a quotation you include in a research paper, then you leave the contraction alone; I am only referring to the use of contractions in sentences you write yourself. Notice that I use contractions in these comments to you. These comments are not a formal essay; they are more like notes from one person to another.

**Verbs, a summary**: It is critical to focus now on the dichotomy between the action verbs and the linking verbs. We will see that this difference is what determines the other parts of sentence and what determines how to use pronouns.

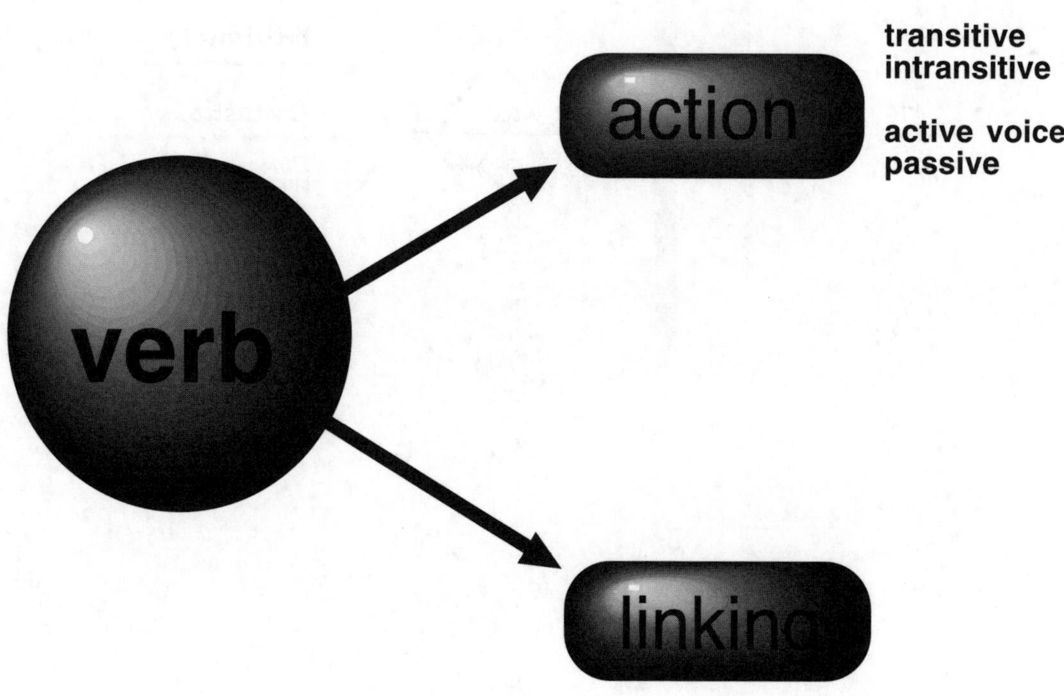

**From Oscar Wilde's *The Picture of Dorian Gray:***

| | He | was | brilliant, | fantastic, | irresponsible. |
|---|---|---|---|---|---|
| **Parts of Speech:** | **pron** | **linking verb** | **adj.** | **adj.** | **adj.** |
| **Parts of Sentence:** | subject | pred. | ----------compound subject complement------------- | | |
| **Phrases:** | no prepositional, appositive, or verbal phrases | | | | |
| **Clauses:** | one independent clause, a simple declarative sentence | | | | |

This sentence by Oscar Wilde shows the power of a linking verb to make an equation. Here, the linking verb lets three adjectives modify the subject pronoun, *he*. He = brilliant, fantastic, irresponsible.

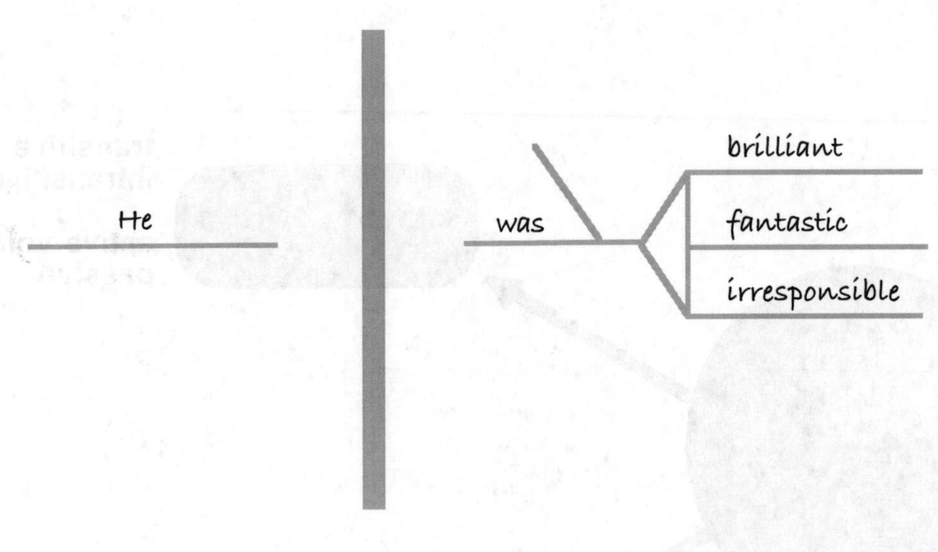

## FOUR-LEVEL ANALYSIS

**From Edgar Allan Poe's *The Pit and the Pendulum:***

| | By | long | suffering | my | nerves | had | been | unstrung. |
|---|---|---|---|---|---|---|---|---|
| **Parts of Speech:** | prep. | adj. | n. (gerund) | pron. | n. | v. | v. | v. |
| **Parts of Sentence:** | | | | | subject | ---predicate (passive voice)--- | | |
| **Phrases:** | no prepositional, appositive, or verbal phrases | | | | | | | |
| **Clauses:** | one independent clause, a simple declarative sentence | | | | | | | |

Poe's sentence is interesting for its gerund as an object of preposition, and for its good passive voice verb; even though the verb is passive, the sentence still has power, with the eerie verb *unstrung* ringing in the silence of the end of the sentence.

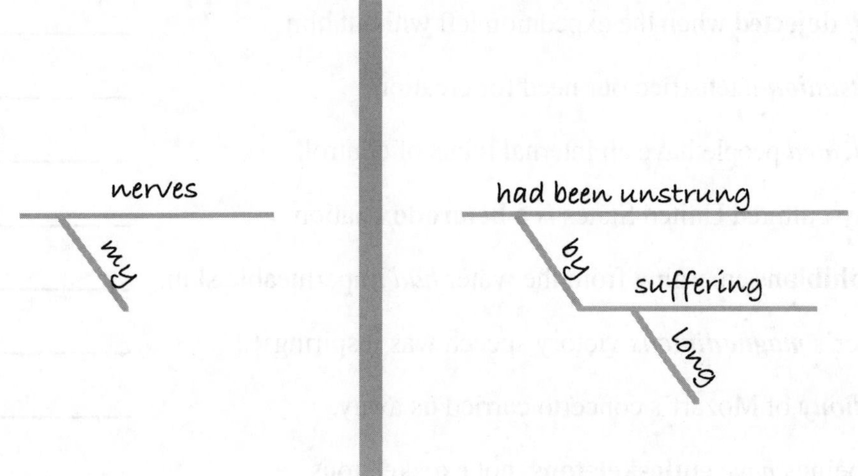

## Verbs from *The Word Within the Word* • List #4

In these sentences, the words in **bold** contain important Latin or Greek stems. Other words are in *italics*. For each word in *italics*, write either *noun*, *adjective*, or *verb* in the blank at the right. If it is a verb, also put *A* for action or *L* for linking.

1. The crystal dissolved into an ***amorphous*** mass. ____________
2. The silk ***vestments*** were hanging on pegs. ____________
3. Pip finally *knew* the name of his generous **benefactor**. ____________
4. The **ponderous** burden *was* nearly impossible to lift. ____________
5. His ***corpulent*** body was a result of his love of sweets. ____________
6. The evil creature *lay* **dormant** for centuries. ____________
7. There *was* a birthday party for the venerable **patriarch**. ____________
8. The recently *invented* laser toothbrush is a **novel** idea. ____________
9. Her ***punctilious*** attention to small details was impressive. ____________
10. Silver *felt* **dejected** when the expedition left without him. ____________
11. The ***devastation*** intensified our need for creation. ____________
12. *Self-motivated* people have an internal **locus** of control. ____________
13. The many-cultured United States *is* a **heterodox** nation. ____________
14. The **amphibians** emerging from the water *had* impermeable skin. ____________
15. Alexander's ***magnanimous*** victory speech was inspiring. ____________
16. The ***euphony*** of Mozart's concerto carried us away. ____________
17. Human beings *have* **endoskeletons**, not exoskeletons. ____________
18. The tremulous dog on the twenty-third floor has ***acrophobia***. ____________
19. The **orthodontist** *straightened* Count Dracula's fangs. ____________
20. The massive **megalith** *towered* over the ancient ruins. ____________

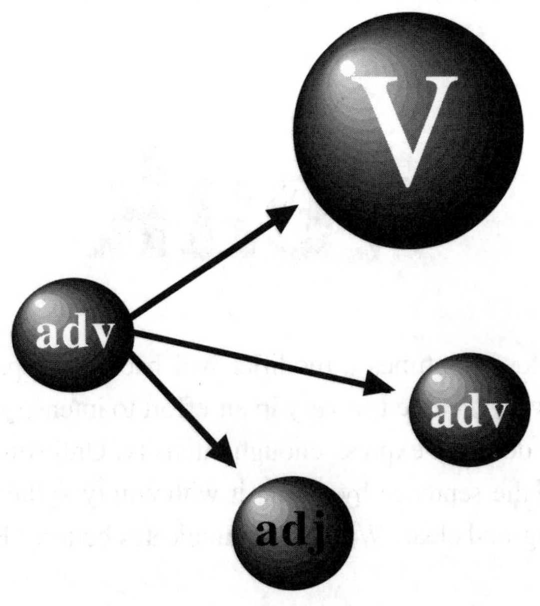


**ADVERB**

**A word that modifies a verb, an adjective, or another adverb.**

**Adverb**: (adv.) An adverb is a word that modifies a verb, adjective, or adverb. Adverbs, please notice, modify three kinds of words that adjectives do not modify. Queequeg swam *slowly*. Ahab is *too* tall. I like you, *too*. He and she swim *well*.

**The Crayola Syndrome**: Mark Twain wrote, "If you see an adjective, kill it." In using modifiers (adjectives and adverbs), you should ask yourself if you are using too many. Though there are wonderful adjectives and adverbs, there are also many that are tired and unnecessary. It is possible you are using tired modifiers because your vocabulary is weak. Are you saying, "bright yellowy green" when you mean *chartreuse*, or are you writing, "light sky blue" when you mean *azure*? Would you describe something as a "very tall, gigantic statue" because you do not know the word *colossus*? Monitor your use of adjectives and adverbs to make sure you are not using clouds of modifiers to compensate for a weak vocabulary. This should not be taken as an endorsement of pompous or stilted language, which is a different way to use words unpleasantly.

Look at this sentence, found on the Internet:

**"During the first half of the twentieth century the world greatly changed."**

Remove the useless adverb *greatly*, and you get a strong sentence, ending in two stressed syllables: "During the first half of the twentieth century, the **world changed**."

**Very, very, very weak**: Sometimes a modifier will backfire, especially when it is overused. One example is the adverb *very*. People use *very* in an effort to intensify adjectives, especially when they sense that the adjective does not express enough intensity. Unfortunately, the adverb *very* often has the effect of weakening the sentence by filling it with empty syllables. Omit the *verys*, and let the adjective stand out strong and clear. Which communicates better: "He was very, very hungry" or "He was hungry"?

The adverb
is not
your friend.
- Stephen King

**Stephen King** has written that "The adverb is not your friend." What do you think he meant?

**Adverbs in Herman Melville's *Moby Dick*:** In his 1851 novel *Moby Dick*, about Captain Ahab and the white whale, Herman Melville used adverbs to modify his verbs, giving an expanded sense of action and event. We see adverbs such as *ere*, *diabolically*, *obstreperously*, *anomalously*, *irrevocably*, *jocularly*, *fain*, *aesthetically*, *palpably*, *vicariously*, *philologically*, *profoundly*, *indolently*, *circumspectly*, *peremptorily*, *obliquely*, *adroitly*, *suffusingly*, *ruefully*, *treacherously*, *intemperately*, *punctiliously*, *impregnably*, *vivaciously*, *sagaciously*, and *ostentatiously*. Do you know all of these adverbs? Which one do you like best?

## Adverbs from *The Word Within the Word* • List #5

For each sentence, identify the part of speech of the word in *italics.*

1. In the spring of 2215, New York was a ***revitalized*** city. ________________
2. The theory of ***democracy*** was proven very effective. ________________
3. If there is ***stereophonic*** sound, can there be stereo smell? ________________
4. Is ***capitalism*** the opposite of Marxism? ________________
5. The poet was traveling ***incognito*** to avoid recognition. ________________
6. The economic disasters could not be *readily* **surmounted.** ________________
7. The senator's **sonorous** voice was *easily* her best weapon. ________________
8. If the **asteroid** struck *the* earth, it would be a **disaster.** ________________
9. Her **dynamic** personality made her an *obvious* choice. ________________
10. Please **synchronize** your chronometers *immediately.* ________________
11. The *very* hyperactive child suddenly began to **hyperventilate.** ________________
12. The astronomer was an ***amiable*** individual. ________________
13. The ***octarchy*** unanimously decided to invade Macedonia. ________________
14. The dancers' spinning **gyrations** *continued* long into the night. ________________
15. Their **contradictory** remarks *really* offered a sharp contrast. ________________
16. Which do you *prefer*, geography or **geophysics**? ________________
17. Galileo thought that the solar system was ***heliocentric***. ________________
18. The **thermotropic** plants were *suddenly* killed by the cold front. ________________
19. Is a *square* a tetragon or just a **tetrahedron**? ________________
20. The **hydrometer** *accurately* measured the flow of the trout stream. ________________

PRE ..................................... POST

**over the rainbow**

**PREPOSITION**

**A word that shows the relationship between its object and another word in the sentence.**

**Preposition**: (prep.) A preposition shows a relationship between its object (the object of the preposition) and another word in the sentence. Prepositions show relationships of time (*before*, *during*, *after*), space (*in*, *on*, *beside*, *around*), and direction (*to*, *from*, *toward*). In other words, prepositions show where two things are located, compared to each other. Prepositions give language its geometry. They are the x,y,z coordinates of the mind. The sphere is *inside* the cube. The beep was *before* the boom. (Or for that matter, the prolegomenon was *before* the epilogue.)

Notice that prepositions are like signs in mathematics, they are small and common, but powerful. To use the wrong preposition is to completely alter the meaning of the idea by changing the relationship between things: would you rather there be a thousand-dollar check *for* you, or a thousand-dollar check *from* you? Like signs in mathematics, prepositions must be used with precision if ideas are to be accurate. Prepositions are called ***pre*** positions because they come at the beginning of the prepositional phrase; they have the PRE position in the phrase: *in* the boat, *on* the dock, *around* Venus.

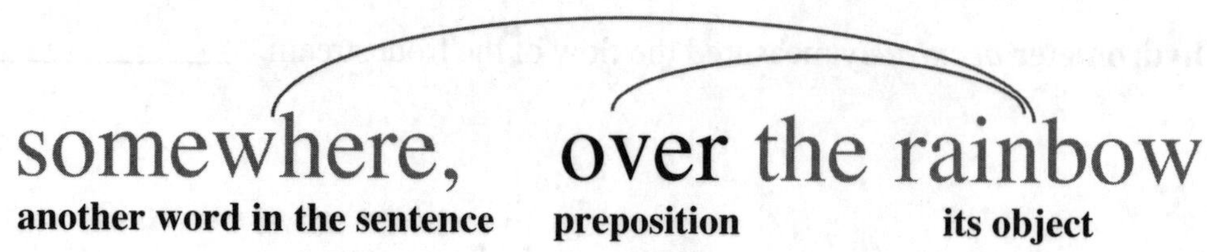

## From Kenneth Grahame's *The Wind in the Willows:*

| | The | rat | only | snorted | and | thrust | his | hands | deep | into | his | pockets. |
|---|---|---|---|---|---|---|---|---|---|---|---|---|
| **Parts of Speech:** | adj. | n. | adv. | v. | conj. | v. | pron. | n. | adv. | prep. | pron. | n. |
| **Parts of Sentence:** | | subject | | --compound predicate-- | | | | direct object | | | | |
| **Phrases:** | | | | | | | | | | prepositional phrase | | |
| **Clauses:** | | | one independent clause, a simple declarative sentence | | | | | | | | | |

Kenneth Grahame uses a prepositional phrase *into his pockets* in this descriptive sentence about the rat. The preposition is *into* and the object of the preposition is *pockets*. *Into* relates *pockets* to some other word in the sentence. Since prepositional phrases are like big adjectives or adverbs, what word do you think the prepositional phrase modifies?

**Never end a sentence with a preposition?** Well, we used to say that. We still deplore such sentences as, "Where are you *at*?" because the meaning of the preposition is incomplete. We want the speaker to finish the idea: Where are you, at home? Where are you, at work? Or we want the speaker to omit the superfluous preposition: "Where are you?" In other cases, however, a concluding preposition does not jar the ear as it once did: "Who is this present for?" is a sentence that would probably not injure the reputation of an educated speaker, even though the stricter "For whom is this present?" is preferred by some. The word *whom* sounds stuffy and inappropriately formal to many people, and it is often avoided with constructions such as, "Who did you go to the theater with?" It is probably still best to follow prepositions with their objects when you can, thus maintaining the logical sequence of the prepositional phrase, as long as it is gracefully possible to do so.

# Where are you, **at....**

**There were some things Winston Churchill would not put up *with*:** After receiving a Minute issued by a civil servant, objecting to the ending of a sentence with a preposition and the use of a dangling participle in official documents, Winston Churchill returned it with this comment, red-penciled in the margin; what do you think Churchill's point was?

# This is the sort of pedantry up with which I will not put.

## Prepositions from *The Word Within the Word* • List #6

For each sentence below, identify the part of speech of the word in *italics*.

1. His irrelevant comments were not **germane** *to* the discussion. ________________
2. The friendly alien proved to be *well-mannered* and **gregarious**. ________________
3. The mariner steered *through* beautiful **ultramarine** waters. ________________
4. The anthropologist loved ***primates***, most of the time. ________________
5. The **pyromaniac** loved starting fires *with* pyrogenic materials. ________________
6. The loudmouth's ***clamorous*** cries could be heard for blocks. ________________
7. The candidate received a **plurality** but not a majority *of* votes. ________________
8. The job has many ***tangible*** benefits for a young person. ________________
9. The regulations were *too* **stringent** for the footloose, creative artist. ________________
10. Did the Emancipation Proclamation ***liberate*** the slaves? ________________
11. There was a jungle *near* the **junction** of the Brazilian highways. ________________
12. Would you rather be **excluded** *from* the new group? ________________
13. There was a decision to **secede** *from* the Union. ________________
14. The Amazon has many **tributaries** flowing *into* it. ________________
15. Don't **dignify** his unworthy question *with* an answer. ________________
16. Your **lucid** remarks clarified the confusing issue *for* everyone. ________________
17. The ***eruption*** of Vesuvius disrupted our celebration. ________________
18. The man *beside* him was certainly no **ingrate**. ________________
19. For Cicero, it was a **mediocre** speech, neither *excellent* nor poor. ________________
20. The **translucent** material allowed us to see on it's *other* side. ________________

## CONJUNCTION

**A word that joins two words or two groups of words.**

**Conjunctions conjoin**: (conj.) A conjunction is a word that joins (*junct*) two words or two groups of words (such as two phrases or clauses) together (*con*). Hamlet *and* Ophelia were here *or* there, *but* we were *and* were not.

**Coordinating conjunctions co-ordinate:** Coordinating conjunctions join equals; they are conjunctions that *coordinate* (join two words or groups of words of similar (co) importance). It is essential that you have the coordinating conjunctions memorized, because you need to know them in order to identify and punctuate compound sentences. The coordinating conjunctions are *and*, *but*, *or*, *nor*, *for*, *so*, *yet*.

**Subordinating conjunctions subordinate:** Subordinating conjunctions join unequals; they are conjunctions that *subordinate*; they join something of lesser importance to something of greater importance. Examples: *if*, *as*, *since*, *when*, *because*, and many others.

I am **and** you are.

I am **when** you are.

**Think of it this way:** In engineering we draw designs for joining things together, but we can join them in different ways, and for different purposes. For example, we might use a fixed joint, or we might use a hinge. Either option gives us a joint, but they are not the same. Conjunctions are like this. A coordinating conjunction **co**-orders what it joins, and a subordinating conjunction **sub**-orders what it joins. A good example is the difference between a compound sentence joined by a coordinating conjunction and a complex sentence joined by a subordinating conjunction. In "Dickens had one idea, *and* his wife had another," both ideas are important, but in "Dickens went to America *when* he had the chance," the second idea only helps to support the first. In using conjunctions, it is necessary to use the right one, the one that agrees with the truth of the idea.

**Correlative conjunctions:** The correlative conjunctions are the multiple-word conjunctions, such as *either/or* and *neither/nor*. *Either* you *or* I will arrive.

**Conjunctive adverbs**: Conjunctive adverbs are conjunctions that act both as adverbs and as conjunctions. These include words that are commonly used to begin clauses, such as *however*, *furthermore*, *moreover*, *nevertheless*, *accordingly*, and *therefore*.

**memorize**

COORDINATING CONJUNCTIONS

**and, but, or, nor, for, so, yet**

SUBORDINATING CONJUNCTIONS

**if, as, since, when, because, .....**

## FOUR-LEVEL ANALYSIS

**From William Shakespeare's *Macbeth:***

| | Fair | is | foul, | and | foul | is | fair. |
|---|---|---|---|---|---|---|---|
| **Parts of Speech:** | n. | v. | adj. | **conj.** | n. | v. | adj. |
| **Parts of Sentence:** | subject | pred. | subject complement | | subject | pred. | subject complement |
| **Phrases:** | no prepositional, appositive, or verbal phrases | | | | | | |
| **Clauses:** | ----independent clause---- | | | | ----independent clause---- | | |
| | two independent clauses, a compound declarative sentence | | | | | | |

This is an extraordinary sentence, dazzling in its elegance. The trick is that it is a mirrorlike compound, two sets of linking verb equations, with the subjects and subject complements reversing, which causes each to change part of speech!

## Conjunctions from *The Word Within the Word* • List #7

For each sentence below, identify the part of speech of the word in italics. If it is a conjunction, identify the type.

1. Please **enumerate** *and* explain your reasons. ____________
2. Her character is one of great *personal* **fortitude**. ____________
3. The **osteologist** was called *in* for consultation or referral. ____________
4. **Ornithology** is a science *for* the bird lovers of the world. ____________
5. **Metropolitan** policy required the police to be polite *but* firm. ____________
6. The stubborn old man *refused* to have the blood **transfusion**. ____________
7. He was *not only* egocentric, *but also* an **egomaniac**. ____________
8. The *ancient* poet was **inspired** by the Muse of poetry. ____________
9. Ralph disputed the dialogue, *so* he received a **diatribe**. ____________
10. The **acrimonious** dispute was *disturbing* to everyone. ____________
11. The culprit was **exculpated** *and* escaped punishment. ____________
12. A **pachyderm** *rarely* suffers from dermatitis on its trunk. ____________
13. *When* it opens, will the zoo have a **protozoan** exhibit? ____________
14. The perforations let water **percolate** *and* pass through the membrane. ____________
15. The **pacifists** were not pacified *by* the militaristic speech. ____________
16. *Neither* **demagogues** *nor* pedagogues are to blame. ____________
17. *If* you have **necrophobia**, avoid the necropolis. ____________
18. *Since* you ask, the wealthy **urbanite** had urbane manners. ____________
19. *Because* he had a **pugnacious** attitude, he was repugnant to others. ____________
20. **Ectothermic** species *and* others enjoy the summer warmth. ____________

## INTERJECTION

**A word shows emotion but has no grammatical function.**

**Interjection**: (interj.) An interjection is a word that shows emotion but has no grammatical purpose. In other words, interjections have no grammar tricks; they do not join, or modify, or show relationships, or replace; they just throw (ject) an exclamation into (inter) the sentence. Interjections are the **Batman words**—words that fill the pages of the action comic books. Examples of interjections are *oh, ugh, oof, wow, yes, no, oops*.

All of the other parts of speech participate in relationships with other parts of speech: a noun agrees with its verb, works with its replacement pronoun, or accepts the modification of its adjective; a verb has its subject and accepts the modification of its adverb; a conjunction joins its words or word groups; an adverb modifies another word. Only the interjection stands alone, thrown (ject) splat! into the sentence. It has less functionality than the other parts of speech, and in this sense the interjection has a certain primitive quality. Perhaps the very first word was an interjection: as the saber-tooth tiger bit the Neanderthal's foot, the Neanderthal might well have interjected, "Rahhrgghh!!" In the beautiful poem "Brown Penny," William Butler Yeats used the interjection *ah*: "Ah penny, brown penny, brown penny, / One cannot begin it too soon."

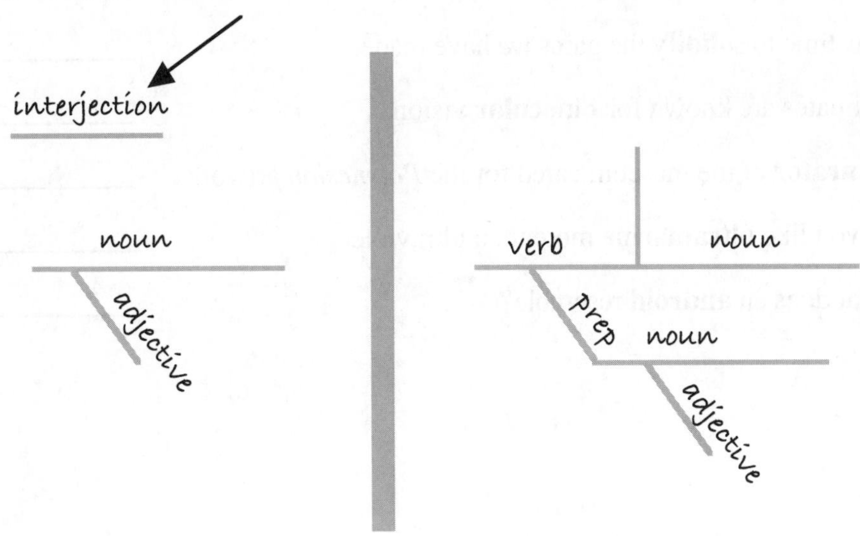

## Interjections from *The Word Within the Word* • List #8

For each sentence, identify the part of speech of the word in italics.

1. *Yes*, his **sedentary** job left him weak and out of shape. ______________
2. The ***illegible*** handwriting said, "Oh, I give up." ______________
3. *Wow*, the bitter animosity made him lose his **equanimity**. ______________
4. No, the ***tortuous*** highway was torture to drive. ______________
5. Yep, NATO, RADAR, *SCUBA*, and OPEC are **acronyms**. ______________
6. Gee, the principles of democracy are ***sacrosanct***. ______________
7. Why, the werewolf is famous for his ***metamorphosis***. ______________
8. *Wow*, the **Petrified** Forest is a desert? ______________
9. *After* the surgery, it was a **miracle** to look in the mirror. ______________
10. After the ***manual*** labor, she needed a **manicure**. ______________
11. *Ugh*! Follow the **directions**, if you want correct answers. ______________
12. Golly, the noisy crowd made ***vociferous*** objections. ______________
13. *Dang*, the **demigod** drank from a dainty demitasse cup. ______________
14. Fooey, the class reunion left me in a ***retrospective*** mood. ______________
15. The explorer could **sense** the edge of the cliff. *Whew*! ______________
16. Yeah, it is time to **solidify** the gains *we* have made. ______________
17. *Nope*, primates are known for **binocular** vision. ______________
18. Oh, the **curator** of the museum cared for the *Polynesian* artwork. ______________
19. *Jeepers*, you like **ultramarine** more than ultraviolet? ______________
20. *Well*, what does an **android** resemble? ______________

**Parts of Speech: an easy system:**

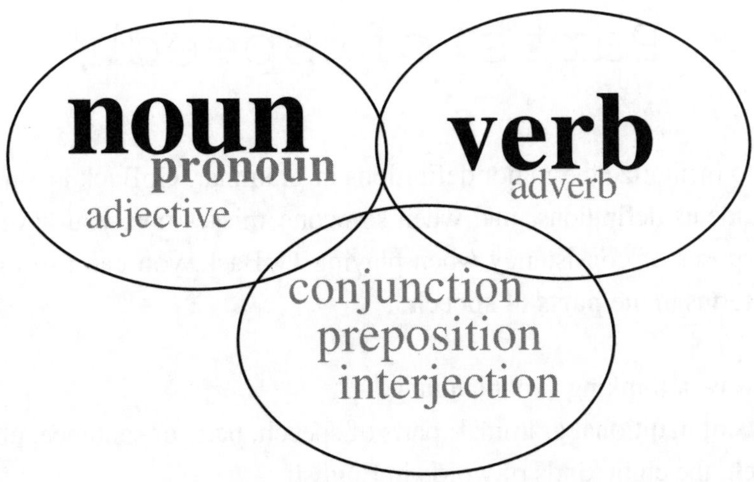


**The Parts of Speech, A Fond Reprise:** In other words (be alert, 'cause I'm going to go fast), **nouns** *name* things; **pronouns** make language *fast*; **verbs** make *events and equations;* **adjectives and adverbs** adjust nouns and verbs; **prepositions** show physics and 3-Dness, **conjunctions** connect; and **interjections** insert emotional excitement.

# **GoBack** definitions

## Level I

## Parts of Speech

It is essential to memorize the major definitions in grammar. GoBack is a memorization game; the teacher asks students definitions, and when someone misses one, you have to go back to the beginning! For purposes of consistency when playing GoBack, you can use these definitions for some of the major terms in the **parts of speech**.

**Grammar**: a way of thinking about language
The **four levels** of traditional grammar: parts of speech, parts of sentence, phrases, clauses
**Parts of speech**: the eight kinds of words in English
**Noun**: the name of a person, place, or thing
**Pronoun**: a word that takes the place of a noun.
**Subject pronouns**: pronouns used for subjects of verbs and subject complements
**List the subject pronouns**: I, you, he, she, it, we, you, they
**Object pronouns**: pronouns used as direct or indirect objects, and objects of prepositions
**List the object pronouns**: me, you, him, her, it, us, you, them
**Adjective**: a word that modifies a noun or pronoun
**Article**: the three adjectives, *a*, *an*, and *the*
**Definite article**: the adjective *the*
**Indefinite articles**: the adjectives *a* and *an*
**Three degrees of adjectives**: positive, comparative, superlative
**Verb**: a word that shows action, being, or links a subject to its subject complement
**Conjunction**: a word that joins two words or two groups of words
**List all the coordinating conjunctions**: and, but, or, nor, for, so, yet
**List a few subordinating conjunctions**: if, as, since, when, because
**The correlative conjunctions**: either or, neither nor, not only but also
**Preposition**: shows the relationship between its object and another word in the sentence
**Interjection**: shows emotion but has no grammatical function

# 2

parts of speech

---

**parts of the sentence**

---

phrases

---

clauses

# Sentences do not occur in nature.

**SENTENCE**

**A group of words that contains a subject and its predicate, and makes a complete thought.**

**Etymology of *sentence***: The word *sentence* comes from the Latin *sententia*, meaning "way of thinking," or "opinion." That is appropriate because the sentence is the structure with which we think about and communicate opinions and ideas.

**Sentence**: A sentence is a two-part thought: it is a group of words that contains a **predicate** about a **subject**, and that makes a complete thought. In other words, a sentence is an idea. "Ishmael watched" is a sentence, but "If Ishmael watched" is not a sentence because we are still waiting for the thought to be completed. If Ishmael watched, then what?

**Parts of the Sentence**: When we study the parts of the sentence, we are studying the structure of thought itself. Sentences do not occur in nature; they are thought, expressed. Hidden in the sentence is thought's secret pattern, and understanding this pattern gives us insight into the nature of clarity. In fact, understanding how sentences are thoughts can give us insight into several different levels of clarity, including clarity of sentence, clarity of paragraph, and clarity of thesis. What is this secret pattern? It is an elegant one: *in order to say anything clearly, we must say two things*. First, we must say what we are talking about, and second, we must say what we are saying about it. Each thought must have these two things.

# 2

**Sentence as paradigm of the mind:** This structure of the sentence shows us a mirror image of our own mind. The sentence, our common one-two structure for building thoughts, gives the mind just what it wants most: a two-piece idea. The two pieces are:

| one | two |
|---:|:---|
| subject | predicate |
| what we're **talking** about | what we're **saying** about it |

The person to whom we are talking needs to know **both**, and if either is absent, unclear, or otherwise disrupted, then we fail to communicate. The sentence is not an extra-human phenomenon of the world, it is made by the mind, it is an extension of the mind itself. In the sentence the mind extends itself out to the world, like an amoeba extending a pseudopod. The sentence is the mind, in language. So we can see the sentence both as a model of how the mind designs its own ideas for transmitting, and we can also see the sentence as a model of how we should write and speak if we want to be understood.

# The sentence *is* the mind, in language.

## FOUR-LEVEL ANALYSIS

**From William Shakespeare's *Julius Caesar:***

| | Cassius | is | aweary | of | the | world. |
|---|---|---|---|---|---|---|
| **Parts of Speech:** | n. | v. | adj. | prep. | adj. | n. |
| **Parts of Sentence:** | subject | pred. | subject complement | | | |
| **Phrases:** | | | | -prepositional phrase- | | |
| **Clauses:** | one independent clause, a simple declarative sentence | | | | | |

This sentence from *Julius Caesar*, like all others, is a two-part thought. The first part is the subject, the one word, *Cassius*. The predicate gives us five words about the subject, and from the predicate we learn that Cassius *is aweary of the world*.

**Clarity at all levels:** This binary form must shape all levels of communication, not just the sentence level. We must know what this **sentence** is about, and what we are saying about it. We must know what this **paragraph** is about, and what we are saying about it. And we must know what this **essay** is about, and what we are saying about it. If the subject or the predicate component is damaged or missing at any of these levels, then one's communication to another person fails.

**SUBJECT**

**The noun or subject pronoun that the sentence is about.**

**Subject**: (subj.) The **simple subject** of the sentence is the noun or subject pronoun that the sentence is about. ***Wittgenstein*** wrote *The Tractatus*. The **complete subject** includes the simple subject and all of its modifiers. *The perspicacious pundit, John Leonard*, excoriated the turgid movie's turbid script. Notice that only subject pronouns (*I, you, he, she, it, we, you, they*) can be sentence subjects. Remember the pronoun rule: a subject is a subject and an object is an object! ***He and I*** entered the competition.

**Compound subject:** A compound subject is a double subject: more than one noun or pronoun used as a double subject of the same clause: *Physics and astronomy* are my favorite subjects. *Einstein and Bohr* debated the quantum theory. A compound subject joined by the coordinating conjunction *and* is considered plural, and must take a plural verb. Jim *and* John *are* here. A compound subject joined by the coordinating conjunction *or* is singular. Jim *or* John *is* here. He *or* she *has* a duck, but he *and* she *have* a lion. Notice how logical this is: if Bach *and* Beethoven wrote symphonies, then two composers wrote, but if Bach *or* Beethoven wrote the *Eroica*, then only one composer wrote it. *And* really is a plural compound, and *or* really is a singular compound. Grammar is logical.

## PREDICATE

**The verb and other words that are about the subject.**

**Predicate**: The predicate is the side of the sentence that says something about the subject. The **simple predicate** is the verb: Hamlet *went* over to the crater at the foot of the escarpment. The **complete predicate** is everything that is said about the subject: Hamlet *went to the crater and gathered three bags of comet dust.*

**Compound verb:** The subject of a sentence may take a compound verb as its predicate. William Blake's famous interrogative complex sentence, in his poem about the tiger, contains a compound verb in the dependent clause: "When the stars threw down their spears / And watered heaven with their tears: / Did He smile His work to see?" The subject *stars* has *threw and watered* as its compound verb. Note Blake's eccentric use of the colon after his dependent clause.

**Subject/predicate set**: The subject/predicate set is the simple combination of simple subject and simple predicate that is *always present as a nucleus in every idea*, in every sentence and in every clause. The sentence or clause may contain more than the subject/predicate set, but it will certainly contain that much. The sentence, remember, is therefore our model of clarity, our model of clear thought. With its subject/predicate set nucleus, the *sentence is a mind-made model of the mind.* In Charles Dickens's famous first sentence to his novel of the French Revolution, *A Tale of Two Cities*, there are sixteen clauses, each with its own subject/predicate set!

It was the best of times, it was the worst of times, it was the age of wisdom, it was the age of foolishness, it was the epoch of belief, it was the epoch of incredulity, it was the season of Light, it was the season of Darkness, it was the spring of hope, it was the winter of despair, we had everything before us, we had nothing before us, we were all going direct to Heaven, we were all going direct the other way—in short, the period was so far like the present period, that some of its noisiest authorities insisted on its being received, for good or for evil, in the superlative degree of comparison only.

- Charles Dickens, *A Tale of Two Cities*

**Ideas have number.** The formal logic of every idea begins with subject/verb agreement. Every sentence is either about something—or about some things! Do you remember that verbs have **number**, that they can be either singular or plural? Well, nouns and pronouns also have number, and will also be either singular or plural. In a sentence, a plural subject must be accompanied by a likewise plural verb (genes transmute), and a singular subject must be accompanied by a likewise singular verb (gene transmutes), or else there is a contradiction (genes transmutes). Both verb and subject indicate number; they express that the sentence is either a thought about something singular, or else it is a thought about something plural. It cannot logically be both. The subject should not tell you that the sentence is about something singular if the verb tells you that the sentence is about something plural. **The number of the subject must equal the number of the predicate**. In other words, you never want the subject and the verb to disagree about whether the subject is singular or plural, even if other distracting and confusing words or phrases come between the subject and its verb. In the following correct sentence, notice how the singular subject and its singular verb agree, ignoring the intervening prepositional phrase: The *top* of the mountains *is* covered by rainbows.

**Español:** In Spanish every sentence has a subject/predicate set, but the subject and its predicate will often be one verb! Of course in English we can have a one-word imperative sentence, such as "Jump!" But the English sentence gives little information about the subject. English verbs do not vary through conjugations significantly: I jump, you jump, he she or it jumps, we jump, you jump, they jump. In Spanish on the other hand, *each person of the verb is different*, and so the verb includes the subject! The Spanish verb *tener* means to have:

| | |
|---|---|
| **tengo**, I have | **tenemos**, we have |
| **tienes**, you have | **teneis** you have |
| **tiene**, he/she/it has | **tienen**, they have |

So whereas in English we could never say, "Has a book," because that would be a sentence **fragment** lacking a subject, in Spanish we can say "Tiene un libro," and the verb will stand alone as a combination subject-predicate! This inclusion of subjects within verbs gives Spanish efficiency and a possibility for emphasis by including a separate pronoun.

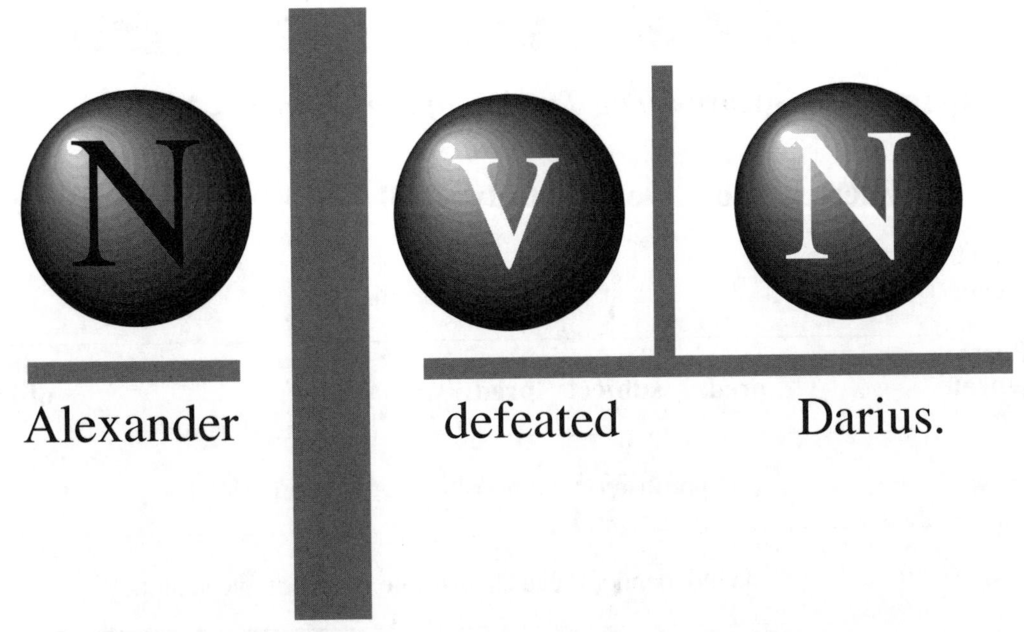


## DIRECT OBJECT

**A noun or object pronoun that receives the action of the action verb.**

**Direct object:** A direct object is a noun or **object** pronoun (*me, you, him, her, it, us, you, them*) that receives the action of the action verb. When there is a direct object, we call the action verb **transitive**; when the action verb does act on a direct object, we call the action verb **intransitive**. Only action verbs can be transitive or intransitive; linking verbs are neither. Notice that subject pronouns may not be used as direct objects, because a subject is a subject. Only an object is an object. The direct object is the object of direct action. We hold these *truths* to be self-evident.

## FOUR-LEVEL ANALYSIS

### From Marjorie Kinnan Rawlings's *The Yearling:*

| | **The** | **sand** | **burned** | **his** | **bare** | **calloused** | **soles.** |
|---|---|---|---|---|---|---|---|
| **Parts of Speech:** | adj. | n. | v. | pron. | adj. | adj. | n. |
| **Parts of Sentence:** | | **subject** | **predicate** | | | | **direct object** |
| **Phrases:** | no prepositional, appositive, or verbal phrases | | | | | | |
| **Clauses:** | one independent clause, a simple declarative sentence | | | | | | |

## FOUR-LEVEL ANALYSIS

**From William Shakespeare's *The Taming of the Shrew:***

| | Where | did | you | study | all | this | goodly | speech? |
|---|---|---|---|---|---|---|---|---|
| **Parts of Speech:** | adv | v. | pron | v. | adj. | adj. | adj. | n. |
| **Parts of Sentence:** | | **pred.** | **subject** | **pred.** | | | | **direct object** |
| **Phrases:** | no prepositional, appositive, or verbal phrases | | | | | | | |
| **Clauses:** | one independent clause, a simple interrogative sentence | | | | | | | |

Here is a fun sentence by William Shakespeare. In Kate's sentence, the subject splits the predicate's helping verb from its main verb, and the direct object is modified by a cascade of adjectives.

Be sure to focus closely on the difference between the direct object and the subject complement, which we will study in a few pages. You need to be able to see, instantly, that your sentence is either an action verb sentence that might have a direct object, or a linking verb sentence that might have a subject complement.

In your mind, keep those two pairs memorized: action verbs with direct objects, and linking verbs with subject complements. The importance of these two pairs will be increasingly clear to you as we learn more.

## INDIRECT OBJECT

**A noun or object pronoun that is indirectly affected by the action verb, and that is located between the action verb and the direct object.**

**Indirect object:** An indirect object is a noun or **object** pronoun located between the action verb and the direct object. The structure is S—AV—**IO**—DO. The indirect object is indirectly affected by the action verb's action on the direct object. Notice that if there is an indirect object, there must be a direct object, and so the action verb is still transitive. We gave *him* the business. Heisenberg gave modern *physics* the Uncertainty Principle.

We use the indirect object as an alternative to using a prepositional phrase. We can either say "The forest brigade gave an ultimatum to the rebels," or we can use the indirect object instead: "The forest brigade gave the rebels an ultimatum."

### FOUR-LEVEL ANALYSIS

**From William Shakespeare's *Hamlet:***

| | **I** | **never** | **gave** | **you** | **aught.** |
|---|---|---|---|---|---|
| Parts of Speech: | pron. | adv. | v. | pron. | n. |
| **Parts of Sentence:** | **subject** | | **action v predicate** | **indirect object** | **direct object** |
| Phrases: | no prepositional, appositive, or verbal phrases | | | | |
| Clauses: | one independent clause, a simple declarative sentence | | | | |

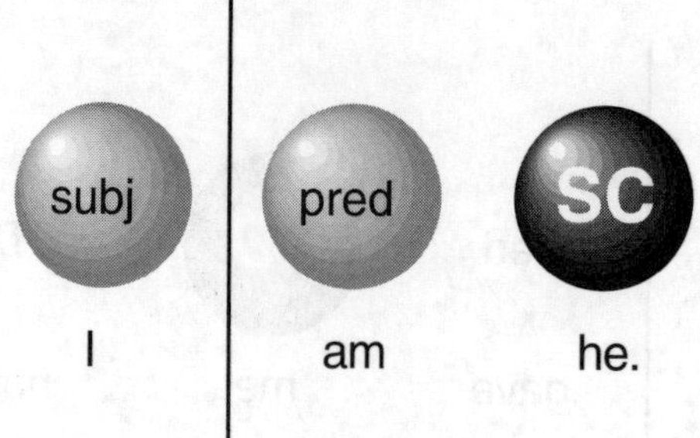


## SUBJECT COMPLEMENT

**A noun, subject pronoun, or adjective that is linked to the subject by a linking verb and tells more about the subject.**

**Subject complement:** A subject complement is a noun, subject pronoun, or adjective that complements the subject; it is linked to the subject by a linking verb. The subject complement, in a sense, renames the subject. Gauguin was Van Gogh's *friend.* Notice that the subject complement does precisely what its name implies; it complements (completes) the subject because it makes our knowledge of the subject more complete than it would otherwise have been. Note that only a subject pronoun can be a subject complement, because a *subject is a subject.*

To compliment someone is to praise him or her; to complement something is to complete it, as the subject complement completes the subject.

### FOUR-LEVEL ANALYSIS

**From William Shakespeare's *Julius Caesar:***

| | It | was | Greek | to | me. |
|---|---|---|---|---|---|
| **Parts of Speech:** | pron. | v. | n. | prep. | pron. |
| **Parts of Sentence:** | subject | predicate | subject complement | | |
| **Phrases:** | | | | -prepositional phrase- | |
| **Clauses:** | one independent clause, a simple declarative sentence | | | | |

This is uttered by Casca in Act I, ii. The linking verb is the basis of the equation.

# compliment
# complement

**Predicate nominative**: *A predicate nominative* is a subject complement that is a noun or subject pronoun. It was *she and I* who came to visit. It is *I*, Hamlet.

**Predicate adjective**: *Predicate adjective* is a term sometimes used to describe a subject complement made out of an adjective. I am *sleepy*.

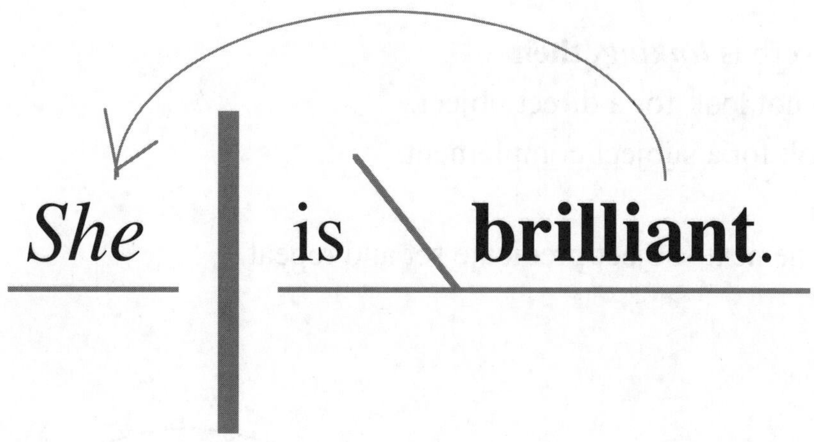


**Why call them "subject complements"?:** I call predicate adjectives and predicate nominatives *subject complements* because it allows me to explain pronoun usage so easily. I can say that anything called a ***subject*** takes a subject pronoun, and anything called an ***object*** takes an object pronoun. **A subject is a subject and an object is an object**. This seems to illustrate the simple truth of pronoun usage. Subjects of verbs and subject complements take subject pronouns.

**Object complement:** An object complement is a noun, object pronoun, or adjective that completes the meaning of the direct object. They elected him *president*. They painted the house *blue*.

**The Boolean (If, then) logic of sentence analysis**: When you analyze the parts of a clause, begin by looking for a one-two thought: a subject/predicate set. Find the subject and its verb. Is the verb action or linking? **If it's an action verb, then** there might be a direct object. If there is a direct object, then look between the direct object and the action verb for an indirect object. **If it's a linking verb, then** there might be a subject complement. Once you have completed the clause, go to the next clause and repeat the process. Everything hinges on whether the verb is action or linking.

## The Logic of Sentence Analysis

**Find the subject/predicate set.**

**Is the verb ACTION or LINKING?**

**If** the verb is ***action*****, then**
Do not look for a subject complement.
Look for a direct object.
**If** you find a direct object, **then**
Look for an indirect object.

**If** the verb is ***linking*****, then**
Do not look for a direct object.
Look for a subject complement.

Look for the next subject/predicate set and repeat.

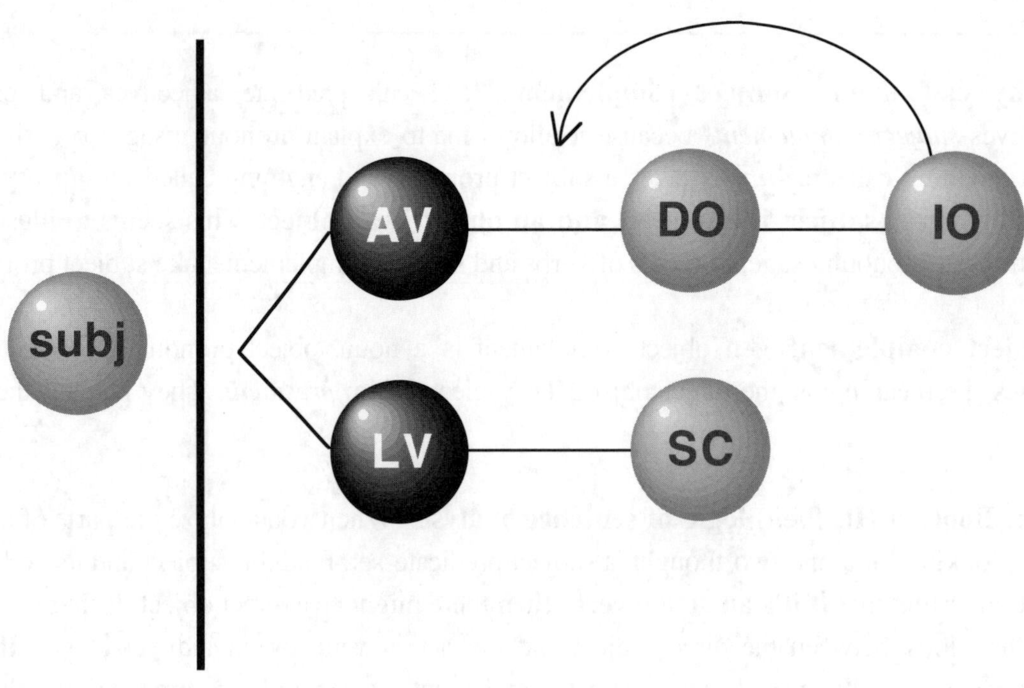

**Wuthering Direct Objects, and Wuthering Subject Complements:** Look at this quotation from Emily Brontë's *Wuthering Heights*, and study the direct objects, which are in bold, and the subject complements, which are circled. See how the direct objects switch pronouns to object case? See that the first subject complement is a predicate nominative, and the second one is a predicate adjective? Can you see how direct objects only go with action verbs, and subject complements only go with linking verbs? Do you realize that you yourself make direct objects, indirect objects, and subject complements all day long, in everything you say and write?

Possibly, some people might suspect **him** of a degree of underbred pride; I have a sympathetic **chord** within that tells **me** it is [nothing] of the sort; I know, by instinct, his reserve springs from an aversion to showy displays of feeling—to manifestations of mutual kindliness....I bestow my own **attributes** over liberally on him. Mr. Heathcliff may have entirely dissimilar **reasons** for keeping his hand out of the way when he meets a would-be **acquaintance**, to those which actuate **me**. Let me hope my constitution is almost [peculiar.]

Now that you understand the parts of the sentence, go back to the parts of speech section and review pronoun usage!

## Parts of the Sentence from *The Word Within the Word* • List #9

In these sentences, each word in **bold** contains important Latin or Greek stems. First, identify the part of speech of the bold word, then identify the part of sentence of the word in italics, using the following abbreviations: subject, subj.; predicate, pred.; direct object, D.O., indirect object, I.O.; and subject complement, S.C. Your blank might look like: adv. D.O.

1. The **pathetic** creature received *sympathy*. __________
2. The unexpected **anomaly** was *amorphous* in shape. __________
3. This is the *difference* between **astronomy** and agronomy? __________
4. Does a **diffident** person have *self-confidence*? __________
5. Does **cacophony** hurt the *ear*? __________
6. The **heterogeneous** mixture had a noisome *odor*. __________
7. Should *science* give us **prescience**? __________
8. Would you like a *photograph* of my **autograph**? __________
9. Is this treaty **bilateral** or *multilateral*? __________
10. The shiny red **tractor** attracted many *buyers*. __________
11. Please **inscribe** *something* insane in my annual. __________
12. *He* refused **to cooperate** with the copilot. __________
13. The **audiophile** has a wonderful *collection* of recordings. __________
14. The **crystalline** *substance* began to evaporate. __________
15. Did the **neolithic** *age* come before the paleolithic age? __________
16. Can you find a *hexagram* and a **hexagon**? __________
17. It's an ***infraction*** of the rules to fracture someone's nose. __________
18. The **platypus** has a plate-like *bill*. __________
19. The Greek **pantheon** of gods was not *monotheistic*. __________
20. Can an ambulatory hospital *patient* **somnambulate**? __________

# **GoBack** definitions

## Level II

## Parts of Sentence

For purposes of consistency when playing **GoBack**, you can use these definitions for some of the major terms in the parts of sentence. Be sure to review the **GoBack** definitions from the Parts of Speech, because the game will be cumulative.

**Sentence**: a group of words that has a subject and its predicate, and makes a complete thought

**Fragment**: an incomplete thought

**Subject**: the noun or subject pronoun that the sentence is about.

**Predicate**: the simple predicate is the verb.

**Direct object**: The noun or object pronoun that receives the action of the action verb.

**Indirect object**: The noun or object pronoun between the action verb and the direct object, that is indirectly affected by the action

**Subject complement**: The noun, subject pronoun, or adjective, that is linked to the subject by a linking verb, and that tells more about the subject.

**Predicate nominative**: A subject complement that is a noun or pronoun.

**Predicate adjective**: A subject complement that is an adjective.

# 3

parts of speech

---

parts of the sentence

**phrases**

---

clauses

# The birds flew over the green treetops.

**PHRASE**

**A group of words without a subject and its predicate, that acts like a single part of speech.**

**Phrase**: A phrase is like a flying formation of birds: it is something made of some things. It is a part of speech made of some words. A phrase is not a complete idea, because it is *a group of words that contains no subject/predicate set and that only acts as a single part of speech.*

We might use a simple adjective in a sentence, or we might use a prepositional phrase instead, or we might use a participle phrase instead. The prepositional and participle phrases give us ways to make the adjective idea more elaborate, more developed.

A government
of the people,
by the people,
and for the people...

**Difference between phrase and clause**: Both phrases and clauses are groups of words, but a clause contains both a subject and its predicate, and a phrase does not. *I jumped* is a clause; *in the boat* is only a phrase. Phrases are found inside clauses; they are part of clauses.

Clauses have **subjects and predicates**.
Phrases **don't**.

## APPOSITIVE

### An interrupting definition.

**Appositive phrase**: An appositive is an interrupting definition. Typically, an appositive defines a noun, and thus forms an adjective. It is called an *appositive* because it is put (pos) beside (ap) what it defines. It is apposed. The idea of an appositive is, "WE INTERRUPT THIS SENTENCE TO BRING YOU A DEFINITION." An appositive may consist of only one word, or it may consist of an entire phrase. We usually enclose appositives and appositive phrases in commas, unless they are exceptionally short and clear by themselves:

Botticelli, **the Renaissance painter**, painted angels.

My friend **Hamlet** is a woodworking artist.

We always enclose **appositive states** and **appositive years** in commas

Athens, **Greece**, is the site of the Parthenon.

June 20, **1997**, is the date of departure.

**Two commas**: Notice that we put commas before **and after** appositives. Don't forget the second appositive commas, or you wind up with catastrophes in which the appositive becomes the subject of the verb, and the subject often becomes a noun of direct address! The result is ridiculous: Botticelli, the Renaissance painter painted angels. Appositives take two commas or none, unless the appositive is at the end of the sentence: I went to see the dancer, Gelsey Kirkland. The comma can make all the difference in the meaning of the sentence:

Botticelli, **the Renaissance painter painted angels.**

**Botticelli,** the Renaissance painter, **painted angels.**

**Prepositional phrase**: A prepositional phrase begins with a preposition (in the PRE position) and concludes with the **object of the preposition**. The preposition relates its object to another word in the sentence. If I say *the dog in the boat*, the preposition *in* shows a spatial relationship between its object *boat* and the noun *dog*. Prepositional phrases behave as modifiers; that is, they act like big adjectives or big adverbs. In the sentence, *The dog in the boat barked*, the prepositional phrase *in the boat* acts as an adjective to modify the noun *dog*.

**The object of the preposition**: The object of the preposition must be a noun or *object* pronoun (*me, you, him, her, it, us, you, them*). A subject is a subject and an object is an object. It is correct to say, "This is a present for you and me," but it is wrong to say "This is a present for you and I." Notice the object pronouns in the following correct prepositional phrases:

**This letter is *for him and me.***

**She and I went *with you and him.***

**I asked a question *about her and us.***

**There is no subject of preposition!** It is not unusual for someone to make the mistake of using subject pronouns as objects of prepositions, especially when the object of preposition is compound. And so someone who would never say, "This remuneration is for I" will mysteriously and ridiculously say "This remuneration is for you and I." But we should always say for *me*: "This remuneration is for you and me" is correct grammar. An object is an object, period. Only object pronouns may be used as objects of prepositions, compounds notwithstanding.

She wrote this poem **for** you and **I**.

She wrote this poem **for** you and **me**.

**Adjective prepositional phrases**: Prepositional phrases that modify nouns or pronouns should be placed immediately after the noun or pronoun they modify. Otherwise, the phrase will be understood to modify the verb. Think through the logic of the following sentence: "On the beach, the dog barked at the **dog** *in the boat*." In "Hokku Poems" Richard Wright wrote, "With a twitching nose / A dog reads a telegram / On a wet tree trunk." Notice that this principle of placement means that no prepositional phrase at the beginning of a sentence can possibly modify a noun or pronoun.

mm

**Misplaced modifiers:** The **mm** proofreader's mark indicates a misplaced modifier, a serious error in grammar. Adjectives, adverbs, prepositional and participle phrases, and even clauses that act as modifiers must be placed next to or as close as possible to the things they modify. If we put the modifier by something else, it will modify something else. The result is often nonsense.

While Isaac **Denisen was chewing her gum**, a fly flew by.

While **chewing her gum, a fly** flew by.

Some more examples: If you say that "In an effort to be modest, Whitman's first edition of poetry lacked his name," that means that the *book* was being modest—a ridiculous idea. To correct the modification error, place the modifier next to the word you really intend to modify: "In an effort to be **modest, Whitman** omitted his name from the first edition of his poetry." The sentence, "An idealist, most of Plato's ideas are only ideals" means that ideas are idealists! Better would have been, "An idealist, Plato regarded his ideas as ideals." "Feeling alone and desperate, this was one of Dinesen's last letters" means that a letter felt desperate. Correct would have been, "Feeling alone and desperate, Dinesen wrote one of her last letters." If you say, "Whitman got to know omnibus drivers and ferryboat pilots at an early age," this could mean that he met very young drivers and pilots. If you put the modifier where it belongs, you get, "At an early age, Whitman got to know omnibus drivers and ferryboat pilots." Modifiers are like lights; they illuminate *things next to them*, and so you have to move them next to their intended targets:

**VERBAL**

**A verb form used as a different part of speech.**

**Verbal phrase**: A verbal is not a verb; it is a former verb now doing something else. Gerunds, participles, and infinitives are the three kinds of verbals. **Gerunds are nouns** (made of verbs); **participles are adjectives** (made of verbs); and **infinitives are nouns or modifiers** (made of verbs). In other words, when we change a verb into a different part of speech, we call it a *verbal*. Verbals are nouns, adjectives, or adverbs made out of verbs.

A verbal can be a single word, or it can join other words to become a phrase. As an example, if I take the verb *was thinking*, and saw off the helping verb *was* so that I only have *thinking* left, I can use this ex-verb as a noun! I can say, "*Thinking is my favorite behavior*." In that sentence, the subject *Thinking* is a verbal, a gerund. It is not yet a verbal phrase. I can make it a verbal phrase by adding words to it: "*Rapidly thinking thoughts is my favorite behavior*."

**Why verbals are fun**: Verbals are fun because they are so creative and energetic. We begin with verbs, and then we make nouns out of them, we make adjectives out of them, we make adverbs out of them, we saw off their helping verbs, and we devise quick ways to express things that would otherwise take paragraphs. Verbals are *not verbs* in sentences, they are ex-verbs, but they still have a verby quality, a verbiness, which gives them energy and force. With verbals, strange things can happen! Verbals are still verby enough that they can even have their own objects, even when they are being used as nouns! Example: *Brushing his face* was the Bigfoot's hobby. This gerund phrase *Brushing his face* is the subject of the sentence! Notice that *face* is the object of the noun/gerund *Brushing*!

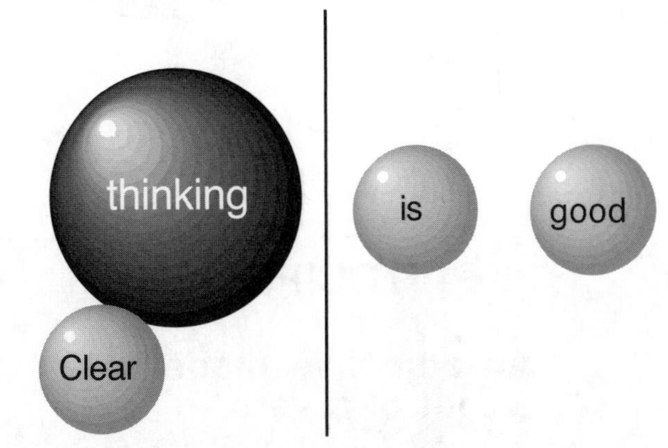


**GERUND**

**A noun made from an -ing verb.**

**Gerund phrase**: A gerund is a **noun** made out of an -ing verb, **or**, an -ing verb made into a noun. (Two ways of saying the same thing.) All kinds of **subjects and objects may be made out of gerunds** or gerund phrases. A gerund might be by itself, or it might join with other words to make a gerund phrase. *Thinking* is fun. *Thinking quickly* is fun. I quit *joking*.

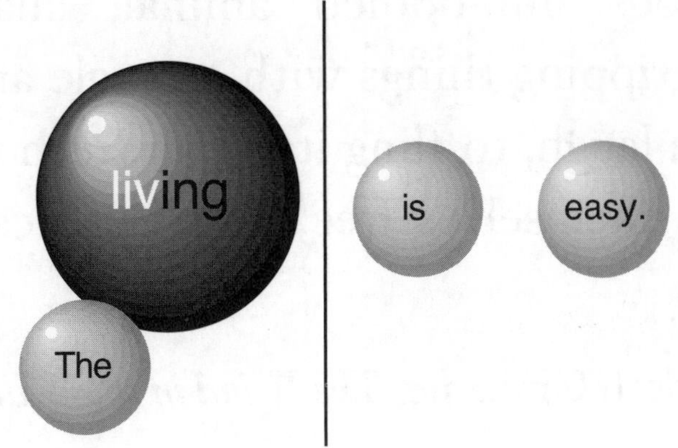

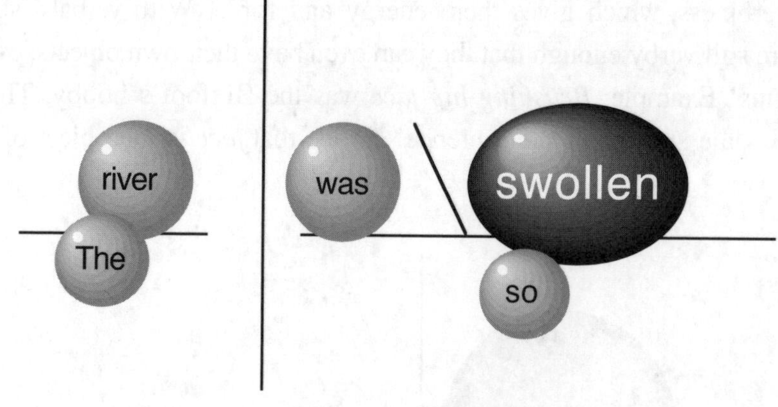


## PARTICIPLE

**An adjective made out of a verb.**

**Participial phrase**: A participle is an **adjective** made out of a verb, **or**, an -ing, -ed, or -en verb made into an adjective. (Two ways of saying the same thing.) Participles always act as adjectives to modify nouns or pronouns. A participle might be by itself, or it might join with other words to make a participial phrase. In the model above, the partciple *swollen* is the subject complement, and since it is modified by an adverb, it is a participial phrase. In *The Wind in the Willows*, Kenneth Graham describes "the swollen river"; do you see the participle in that sentence? Is it a participial phrase? Yeats used participles in his poem "The Second Coming": "Turning and turning in the widening gyre / The falcon cannot hear the falconer." Look at this sentence from *The Wind in the Willows*, and see how many participles you can find:

> Never in his life had he seen a river before—this sleek, sinuous, full-bodied animal, chasing and chuckling, gripping things with a gurgle and leaving them with a laugh, to fling itself on fresh playmates that shook themselves free, and were caught and held again.
>
> - Kenneth Grahame, *The Wind in the Willows*

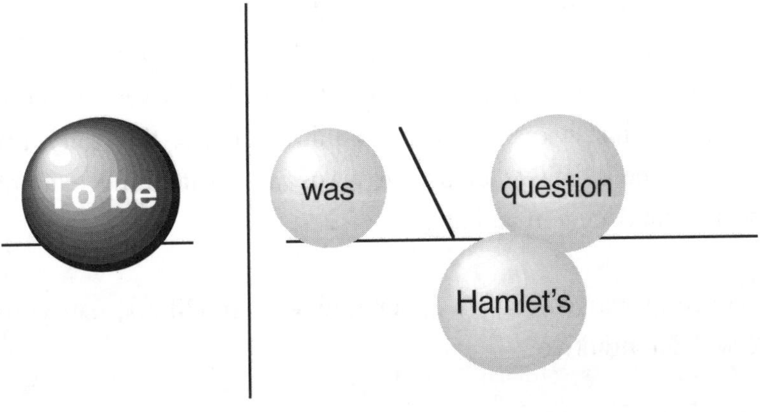


## INFINITIVE

**A noun or modifier made from the to- form of the verb.**

**Infinitive phrase**: An infinitive is a general form of the verb made into a **noun**, **adjective**, or **adverb**. This general form of the verb is usually expressed by beginning with the word *to*: to think, to dream, to snorkle, to excoriate. The infinitive is named for the fact that it is not (in) limited (fin) in tense/time. Since the infinitive is not limited to a tense, it is never used as a true predicate; we do not say, for example, "I to go home." Examples of infinitives include: *To think* is a pleasure. (noun) The philosopher *to read* is Plato. (adjective) He lives *to fish.* (adverb) To be is the question.

**To be or not to be = 4 words!**

***To Think* is one word:** We think of an infinitive as *one word.* In our four-level analysis, the infinitive *to wander* is a single word, whereas a prepositional phrase like *to Boston* is two words.

Since an infinitive is only one word, it is best to word your sentences as to **avoid split infinitives**. Splitting an infinitive means inserting an adverb between the two words of the infinitive. If we take the infinitive *to see*, and split it with the adverb *vividly*, we have *to vividly see*, which is a split infinitive. It is better to put the adverb after the infinitive: to see vividly.

Split infinitives are hard **to ~~really~~ understand**.

**The anomalous infinitive clause**: Here is an exception to our "a subject is a subject and an object is an object" rule. It is also an exception to the idea that all predicates must have tense. This structure is known as the *infinitive clause*. It is actually possible for an infinitive to act as the predicate of an object pronoun, even though only subject pronouns usually take predicates! An example of an infinitive clause would be, "We wanted him to eat fish." In this sentence, the word *him* has to serve two purposes; it is the direct object of the main clause, and it is also the subject of the infinitive clause. In other words, when it comes to a showdown over who controls the case of the pronoun, the main clause wins; it overrules the infinitive clause. So really, this exception to the pronoun rule is logical. The infinitive clause gives us an outstanding example of the powerful flexibility and creativity that occurs in language.

**A Question**: Since infinitives can be either nouns or modifiers, can you think of a way to modify an infinitive with an infinitive?

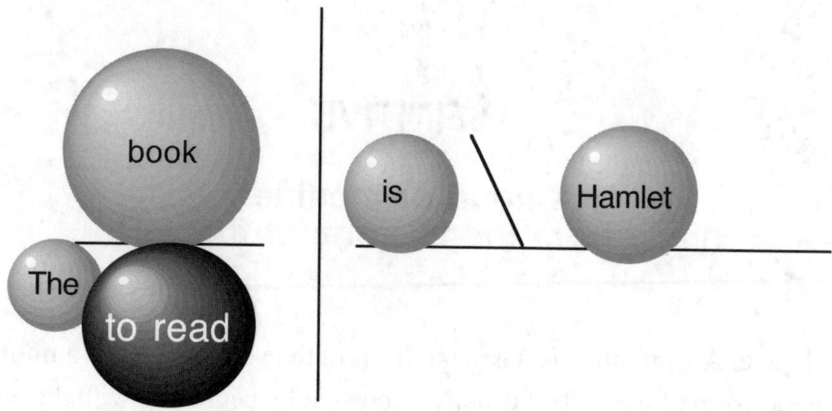


An infinitive can be an adjective. Here it modifies the subject.

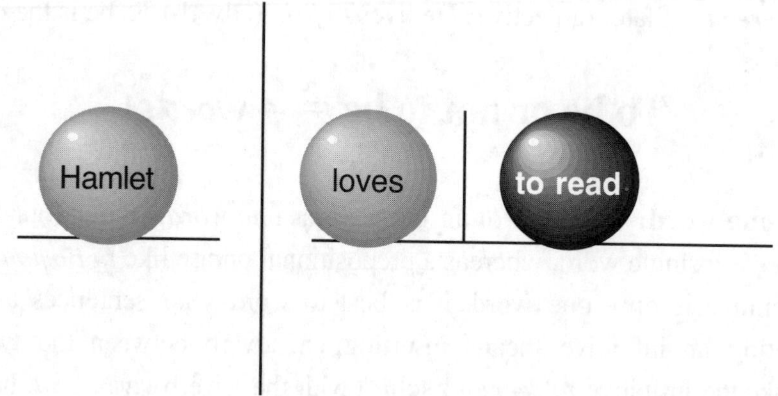


An infinitive can be a noun. Here it is the direct object.

# Summary of Phrases

**Prepositional** phases are modifiers. They act like adjectives or adverbs. The adjective kind has to follow immediately the noun it modifies. We put a comma after multiple introductory prepositional phrases, but not after a single short one. Example: The philosopher *with the hemlock* did not feel thirsty.

• • •

**Appositive** phrases are interrupting definitions, and so the are adjectives. They take two commas or none. Example: Socrates, *the interrogative philosopher*, decided to drink the hemlock.

• • •

**Verbal** phrases are based on verbs that have been adapted to become other parts of speech.

• **Participles** are verbals that act as adjectives. They can end in various verby endings, but they will always be modifying a noun or pronoun. Example: *Shaking* fearfully, the frightened creature looked at the door.

• **Infinitives** are verbals that are nouns or modifiers and that begin with *to*, although sometimes the *to* is only understood to be there. Example: *To think* is fun.

• **Gerunds** are verbals ending in -ing and acting as nouns. A gerund can be the subject of a sentence or the direct object—anything that any noun can be. Example: *Thinking* is fun.

All of the verbals can appear by themselves in a sentence; they only become verbal *phrases* when they are modified by another word or when they have their own object.

## FOUR-LEVEL ANALYSIS

**From Robert Louis Stevenson's *Treasure Island:***

| | The | figure | reappeared | and | began | to head | me | off. |
|---|---|---|---|---|---|---|---|---|
| **Parts of Speech:** | adj. | n. | v. | conj. | v. | ----n.---- | pron. | adv. |
| **Parts of Sentence:** | | subject | --------compound predicate-------- | | | ------direct object ------ | | |
| **Phrases:** | | | | | | **----infinitive phrase----** | | |
| **Clauses:** | | one independent clause, a simple declarative sentence | | | | | | |

This sentence, which has been shortened for brevity, is from *Treasure Island.* It has a nice compound verb as a predicate and also a beautiful infinitive phrase that serves as the direct object of the second verb. Notice that the infinitive, though it is a noun in the sentence, is still verby enough to have its own object, *me*, and to be modified by an adverb! So here, incredibly, we have a noun modified by an adverb!

**Appositive phrase vs. parenthetical remark vs. nonessential clause vs. sharp break in thought**: Students are often confused about how certain kinds of sentence interrupters differ from each other. Though each of these elements could be said to interrupt the sentence, they differ in other ways:

An **appositive phrase** is a *definition* inserted into a sentence: Smee, the rascally pirate, needs a mother.

A **parenthetical remark** is not a definition but a related comment or aside inserted into a sentence: Pirate Smee (How did *he* get into Neverland?) needs a mother.

A **nonessential clause** (See clause discussion below) is an adjective clause beginning with a relative pronoun: Pirate Smee, who probably needs a mother, is Hook's toady.

A **sharp break in thought** is one so unrelated to the sentence that you separate it with dashes: Pirate Smee—Get that alligator off my foot!—needs a mother.

## Phrases from *The Word Within the Word* • List #10

For each of these sentences, first identify the part of speech of the word in **bold**, then identify the kind of phrase that is in italics.

1. The **orthopedist** went *on an expedition.* ______________
2. Dr. Garcia, *the new mortician*, was **mortified** at the wound. ______________
3. The **carnivorous** beasts *of the plains* lived well. ______________
4. The **psychologist** viewed the parapsychologist *with suspicion.* ______________
5. *Contradicting democratic philosophy,* **Ethnocentrism** injures all. ______________
6. The geneticist's hobby was *to study* ***pathogenic*** *substances.* ______________
7. **Prenatal** care is important *to those in natural environments.* ______________
8. The **paleontologist** was an expert *on the Paleozoic era.* ______________
9. To talk glibly gives only **cursory** attention *to the problem.* ______________
10. The **cryptologist** worked all night *to break the enemy code.* ______________
11. *Cracked lengthwise*, the object was discovered near the **cascade**. ______________
12. ***Decapitating*** *criminals* was once a common form of punishment. ______________
13. The **loquacious** bore answered *with a circumlocution.* ______________
14. *From the beginning* the hero's sacrifice was a **sacrosanct** memory. ______________
15. The **United** Planets soon celebrate *forming their union.* ______________
16. The sky's **redness** streamed high *over the Himalayas.* ______________
17. The **altimeter**, *rusted shut*, no longer measured the altitude. ______________
18. Computer **graphics** enhance books *on politics and economics.* ______________
19. The **isothermal** foothills escaped the extremes *of temperature.* ______________
20. The new convert soon **reverted** *to his previous views.* ______________

# **GoBack** definitions

## Level III

## Phrases

For purposes of consistency when playing **GoBack**, you can use these definitions for some of the major terms in the phrases. Remember to review Levels I and II before playing **GoBack**. Also, keep your thinking clear: remember that if you learn what these things are, you will benefit from it all of your life.

**Phrase**: A group of words that does not have a subject and its predicate.
**Prepositional phrase**: A phrase beginning with a preposition, used as a modifier.
**Appositive**: An interrupting definition.
**Verbal**: A verb form used as a noun, adjective, or adverb.
**The three kinds of verbals**: Gerunds, participles, and infinitives.
**Gerund**: An -ing verb form used as a noun.
**Participle**: A verb form of various endings used as an adjective.
**Infinitive**: The *to-* form of the verb, used as a noun or modifier.

parts of speech

parts of the sentence

phrases

**clauses**

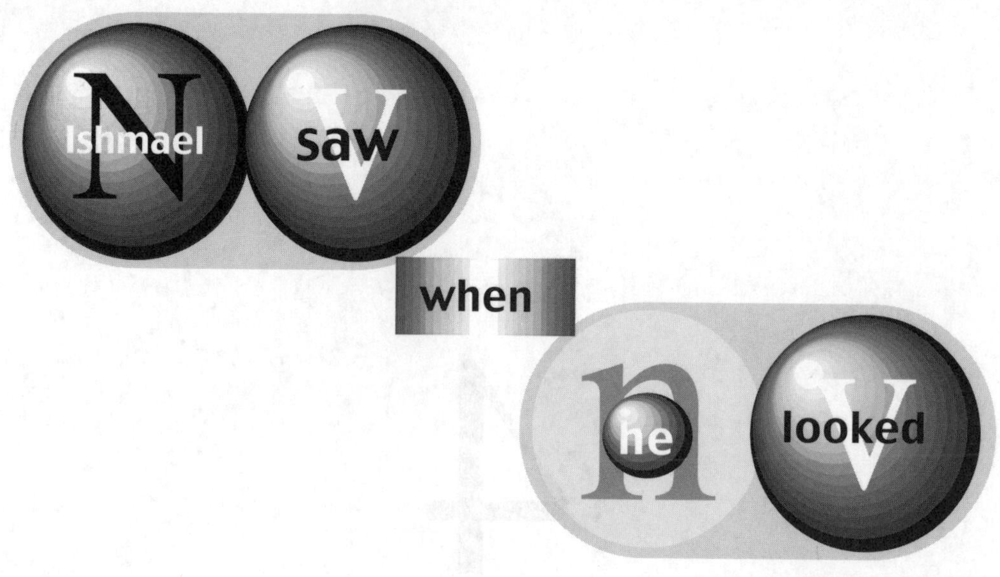


**CLAUSE**

**A group of words that contains a subject and its predicate.**

**Clause that idea**: Clauses are easy. The word *clause* comes from the same root as the words *claustrophobia*, *enclosure*, and *close*. The idea is that a clause is a closing: the subject opens the topic, and the predicate closes it; the subject asks, and the predicate answers. A clause is simply a **group of words that contains a subject *and* its predicate**, and this one-two structure opens and closes an idea. Every clause has this subject/predicate set at its center.

clause

**[subject, predicate]**

open, close

The complete clause includes not only the subject and the verb, but all of the modifiers and phrases that go with them. A sentence might consist of only one clause, or it might contain several clauses, each with its own subject and predicate. How many clauses do you think you see in this passage from Henry David Thoreau's *Walden*?

I desire that there may be as many different persons in the world as possible; but I would have each one be very careful to find out and pursue his own way, and not his father's or his mother's or his neighbor's instead. The youth may build or plant or sail, only let him not be hindered from doing that which he tells me he would like to do.

**I and D—Two Kinds of Clauses:**

**Independent clause (I):** An independent clause is a clause that makes sense independently: *Ibsen was a gadfly.*

**Dependent clause (D):** A dependent (or *subordinate*) clause is a clause that does not make sense unless it can "hang on to" (de-down pend-hang) an independent clause. Dependent clauses are sometimes called *subordinate clauses,* and often begin with subordinating conjunctions. *If Ibsen was a gadfly . . .*

## FOUR-LEVEL ANALYSIS

### From William Shakespeare's *Julius Caesar:*

| | **When** | **Caesar** | **says** | **"Do** | **this,"** | **it** | **is** | **performed.** |
|---|---|---|---|---|---|---|---|---|
| **Parts of Speech:** | conj. | n. | v. | v. | pron. | pron. | v. | v. |
| **Parts of Sentence:** | | subject | predicate | ---- direct object --- | | subj. | --passive voice pred.-- | |
| **Phrases:** | no prepositional, appositive, or verbal phrases | | | | | | | |
| **Clauses:** | **--------------------dependent clause--------------** | | | | | **--------independent clause-----** | | |
| | **a complex declarative sentence** | | | | | | | |

This sentence is unusual because the direct object, *Do this*, of the introductory dependent clause is also a clause! See the subordinating conjunction?

**Adjective dependent clause:** An adjective clause (or relative clause) is a dependent clause used as an adjective: a (usually) short dependent clause that follows a noun or pronoun and modifies it. The adjective clause often interrupts the main clause, dividing the subject from the verb. Adjective clauses begin with relative pronouns. The man *who followed you* turned left. We watched the man *who turned left*. Whitman wrote, "I am he that walks with the tender and growing night."

**The comma chameleon—punctuating essential and nonessential adjective clauses**: Adjective clauses that are important to the meaning of the sentence need no commas around them, but adjective clauses that are unnecessary interruptions should be enclosed in commas. In other words, **if you do need the clause, you don't need the commas, and if you don't need the clause, then you do need the commas. You need one or the other**. If the clause is essential, then the commas aren't. Examples: The man who followed you turned left. The man, who happened to know Humphrey, coughed.

***That*** versus ***which***: Here is a good usage clue. The relative pronoun *that* often indicates an essential adjective clause: The book *that you lost* is on the shelf; whereas the relative pronoun *which* often indicates a nonessential adjective clause: The book, *which I enjoyed too*, is on the shelf.

**Adverb dependent clause**: Adverb clauses are dependent clauses that act as big adverbs. Adverb clauses usually begin with subordinating conjunctions. I jumped *when the fish expanded.*

**Noun dependent clause**: Noun clauses are dependent clauses that act as nouns. In the following sentence, the noun clause acts as a direct object to the action verb *wish*: I wish *that I liked music*.

**Where dependent clauses go:** Dependent clauses can not be used as sentences by themselves; they depend on (hang down from) an independent clause for meaning. The dependent clause may be placed before, after, or even in the middle of an independent clause:

> **If you find the white whale**, the voyage will be a success.
> The evil will collapse **when the white whale is destroyed**.
> The poet **who wrote the cantos** was exiled to Italy.
> I found **what I was looking for**.

**Let's be very Thoreau:** In *Walden*, Thoreau wrote some of the most beautiful sentences in American literature to convey some of the most profound ideas in American history. Look at this passage, and notice some of his dependent clauses, which will be in black. The independent clauses will be in gray: Do you see the subordinating conjunctions subordinating the second two clauses? What kind of dependent clause is the first one?

I am no more lonely than the loon in the pond **that laughs so loud**, or than Walden Pond itself. What company has that lonely lake, I pray? And yet is has not the blue devils, but the blue angels in it, in the azure tint of its waters. The sun is alone, except in thick weather, **when there sometimes appear to be two**, but one is a mock sun...
I have occasional visits in the long winter evenings, **when the snow falls fast** and the wind howls in the wood...

**The difference between clause and sentence:** A clause has both a subject and predicate, like a sentence, but a sentence always has a complete thought, whereas a clause might be incomplete. A sentence can consist of several clauses: If you find the Auden poem, I will scan its meter. In this sentence, there are two clauses; *If you find the Auden poem* is a dependent clause in which *you* is the subject and *find* is the simple predicate, and *I will scan its meter* is an independent clause in which *I* is the subject and *scan* is the simple predicate. So every sentence has at least one independent clause in it, but not every clause is a sentence because a dependent clause does not make a complete thought—it is dependent upon an independent clause.

We could express the relationship between clauses and sentences with Aristotelian syllogisms:

A. All sentences contain at least one independent clause.
B. "All men are created equal" is a sentence.
C. Therefore, "All men are created equal" contains at least one independent clause.

Or,

A. No dependent clause is a sentence by itself.
B. "If you can keep your head" is a dependent clause.
C. Therefore, "If you can keep your head" is not a sentence.

## Four Sentence Structures

In the following discussion of how clauses can be combined into sentences, let the letter *I* stand for the independent clause, and let the letter *D* stand for the dependent clause. Let the letters *cc* stand for the coordinating conjunction (*and, but, or, nor, for, so, yet*).

# I

**Simple sentence**: (Structure: **I**) A simple sentence is a sentence consisting simply of one independent clause. You can use a simple sentence to isolate an idea for attention. In his poem "The Disillusionment of Ten O'Clock" poet Wallace Stevens began with a simple sentence, "The houses are haunted / By white night gowns."

# II

**Compound sentence:** (Structure: **I+I** or **I+I+I**, etc.) A compound sentence is a sentence compounded of two or more independent clauses. You can use a compound sentence to connect two related ideas of equal or nearly equal importance. Punctuate I;I or I,ccI. From Sylvia Plath's poem "The Moon and the Yew Tree": "It drags the sea after it like a dark crime; it is quiet / With the O-gape of complete despair." Randall Jarrell used a compound sentence in his poem "Death of the Ball turret Gunner": "From my mother's sleep I fell into the State, / And I hunched in its belly till my wet fur froze."

# ID D,I

**Complex sentence:** (Structure: **I+D** or **D+I** or **D+I+D**, etc.) A complex sentence is a sentence that is complex because it consists of an independent clause joined to a dependent clause. You can use a complex sentence to show a primary idea that has a lesser idea in support of it. The independent clause will contain the primary idea. Punctuate **D,I** or **ID**. From poet Edward Arlington Robinson: "Whenever Richard Cory went down town, / We people on the pavement looked at him." In his poem "The Darkling Thrush," Thomas Hardy wrote, "I leant upon a coppice gate / When Frost was specter-gray."

# IID DII

**Compound-complex sentence:** (Structure: **I+I+D** or **D+I+I**, etc.) A compound-complex sentence is a sentence that contains both compound clause structure and complex clause structure. You can use a compound-complex sentence to employ the strategies of compound and complex sentences at once. Punctuate a compound-complex sentence two clauses at a time, according to the rules for compound and complex sentences. Poet A.E. Housman wrote, "The time you won your town the race, / We chaired you through the marketplace; / Man and boy stood cheering by, / And home we brought you shoulder-high."

## Summary of clause punctuation:

| | |
|---|---|
| **I,ccI** | (comma before coordinating conjunction in compound sentence) |
| **I;I** | (semicolon between independent clauses if no coordinating conjunction) |
| **ID** | (no comma after independent clause in complex sentence) |
| **D,I** | (comma after dependent clause in complex sentence) |

Note: this easy summary of clause punctuation gives a quick reference for punctuating independent clauses and adverbial dependent clauses. Adjective (relative) clauses are different; the relative clause is enclosed in commas if it is a nonessential interruption to the main idea, but it is not enclosed in commas if its presence in the sentence is essential or necessary.

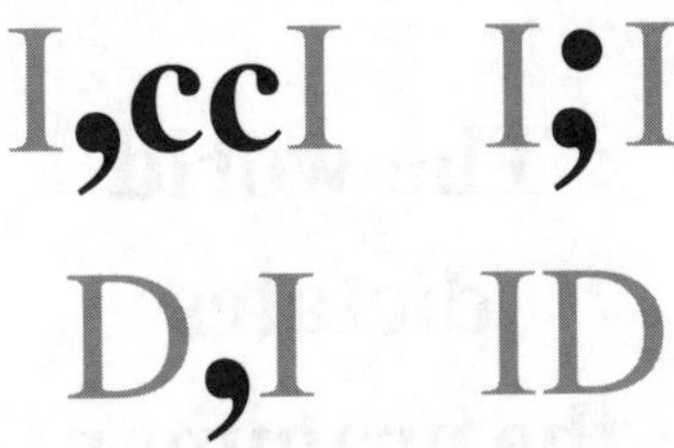


~~IccI~~ run-on!
~~I,I~~ comma splice!

**DI?:** Even though we often teach students to put a comma after the introductory adverbial dependent clause in a **D,I** complex sentence, that comma is often omitted in published material if the sentence seems clear and readable without the comma. The teacher may wish to emphasize to students that at the professional level this comma is regarded as discretionary.

**Comma splice error:** A comma splice is the error of joining two independent clauses with a comma. **(I,I)** The archaeologist went to Cairo, we went home. To correct this error, either insert a coordinating conjunction after the comma, or change the comma to a semicolon.

**Run-on sentence error:** A run-on sentence is the error of joining two independent clauses with only a coordinating conjunction or with nothing. (**IccI** or **II**) This causes the two ideas in the compound sentence to blur together, losing their clear identities. The archaeologist went to Cairo but we went home. The archaeologist went to Cairo we went home. Remember that poets and novelists will sometimes deliberately use run-on sentences; Wallace Stevens did in his sentence, "The house was quiet and the world was calm." Ernest Hemingway was famous for it.

**Four Purposes of Sentences/Ideas**:

The sentence purposes are so well named that they are virtually self-defining. Each does precisely what its name implies:

> **declarative sentence:** A declarative sentence is a sentence that *declares* (states). I will.
>
> **interrogative sentence:** An interrogative sentence is a sentence that *interrogates* (asks). Will you? T.S. Eliot's J. Alfred Prufrock asked, "Do I dare to eat a peach?"
>
> **imperative sentence:** An imperative sentence is a sentence that *imperiously* commands. Go away. Dylan Thomas wrote, "Do not go gentle into that good night."
>
> **exclamatory sentence:** An exclamatory sentence is a sentence that *exclaims*. I will!

# The world dictates the grammar.

**The world dictates the grammar.** Grammar serves meaning, and not conversely. You cannot seek within grammar for the all causes of grammatical structure; these causes are often external. A sentence will not be simple, complex, or compound because of the rules of grammar; it will have clause structure suitable to the ideas.

There may be short, simple sentences because the moment to be communicated—say, Cornwall's dying gasps in Shakespeare's *King Lear*— requires a series of terrible silences, that position themselves tragically *between* the sentences: "I have received a hurt. Follow me, lady. Turn out that eyeless villain; throw this slave upon the dunghill. Regan, I bleed apace. Untimely comes this hurt; give me your arm." There is nothing, internal to grammar, which dictates the use of these staccato, clipped sentences; rather, it is Cornwall's pain, his inability to utter more than a few words at a breath, which explains the syntax. Cornwall has been stabbed, and in his only thirty-one wounded words there are seven clauses, five periods, two commas, and two semicolons. The passage has an average of only four words per clause. It is not Cornwall's words that communicate his agony, but rather the *interwords* that dictate his constricted grammar, forcing itself into the gaps between his death spasms:

> "I have received a hurt/////////////Follow me////////////////lady////////////////Turn out that eyeless villain////////////throw this slave upon the dunghill///////////////Regan////////////I bleed apace//////////////////// Untimely comes this hurt////////////////////give me your arm."

Clearly, the secret of Cornwall's grammar cannot be internally analyzed within the system of grammar itself; the grammar is not a function of itself but of the character's experience: his small gasps of sentence are all he can manage between his large gasps of death.

The example of Cornwall vividly illustrates another insufficiently contemplated aspect of language study, the extraordinary meaning and power of punctuation. In every period and comma of Cornwall's death there is an abyss.

**I have received a hurt.**

**Follow me, lady.**

**Turn out that eyeless villain.**

**throw this slave upon the dunghill.**

**Regan, I bleed apace.**

**Give me your arm.**

# **GoBack** definitions

## Level IV

For purposes of consistency when playing GoBack, you can use these definitions for some of the major terms in the clauses. Be sure to review the definitions from the first three levels.

**Clause:** A group of words that has a subject and its predicate.

**Independent clause:** A clause that is a complete thought.

**Dependent clause:** A clause that is not a complete thought, but needs to be connected to an independent clause.

**The four clause structures:** Simple, compound, complex, compound-complex.

**Simple sentence:** A sentence with one independent clause.

**Compound sentence:** A sentence with two or more independent clauses.

**Complex sentence:** A sentence with an independent clause attached to a dependent clause.

**Compound-complex sentence:** A sentence with a compound structure and a complex structure.

**The four sentence purposes:** declarative, imperative, interrogative, exclamatory.

**Declarative sentence:** A sentence that declares or makes a statement.

**Imperative sentence:** A sentence that is imperious, that makes a command.

**Interrogative sentence:** A sentence that interrogates, that asks a question.

**Exclamatory sentence:** A sentence that exclaims, that has an exclamation point.

**Review**: As a way to review, try inventing an alien grammar. Create a language like English, except that 5-10 of the rules are different. Here is a sample:

# Alien Grammar

Your ship crashes and you find yourself in a strange, alien land, with green clouds and yellow mountains. Navy blue streams traverse the landscape, and pink fish jump from the water. A crisp, cool wind blows the mauve trees to the west, or is it the east? The three suns shine down from the crimson sky, casting a triple shadow. Strange, yes, but the strangest part is yet to come: the grammar.

In this land, the language is just like English, except that certain rules are different. For example:

1. Singular nouns all end in -lo, and plural nouns all end in *-lolo,* not *-s.* The subject complement suffix is attached after the singular/plural suffix.
2. Adjectives immediately follow nouns, and end in *-la.*
3. Adverbs immediately follow what they modify, and end in *-loo.*
4. The first word of every sentence is the verb, unless the sentence is interrogative. Verbs begin with the hissing sound *sss-.*
5. There are no object pronouns, only subject pronouns; everything is thought to be alive.
6. All subject pronouns begin with the prefix *lee-*
7. Direct objects and objects of verbals begin with the prefix *lum-.*
8. Subject complements begin with *lim-* and end with *-mil.*
9. The preposition begins with the prefix *ner-* is the last word of the prepositional phrase.
10. Interrogative sentences begin with the word *hooop.*
11. The second person pronoun is never spoken, out of respect. This missing word is indicated by the humming sound, *mmmm.*
12. The definite article is *rach* and the indefinite article is *roop.*

As you gaze around in mute stupefaction, a creature flops flappily across the ground to you, peers intensely into your eyes, his nose almost touching yours. He blinks, and says in Floppy:

**Hooop sssare what rach hecklo limmmmmmil. Ssssaw neverloo beforeloo leeI lumanythinglo strangela soloo as mmmm. Hooop sssare mmmm roop limmonsterlomil. Hooop sssis why mmmm noselo mmmm eyelolo nirbelow. Ssshave leeI lumscalelolo nicela tummylo myla neron. Hooop ssswould ssslike mmmm to pat lumheadlo myla.**

Translate the alien's language into ordinary English. Then translate a well known saying in English into Floppy. You might choose a famous paragraph from a historical document, or a humorous dialogue in a television commercial.

---

What the heck are you? I never saw anything so strange as you before. Are you a monster? Why is your nose below your eyes? I have nice scales on my tummy. Would you like to pat my head?

# Punctuation Rules
# A Concise Summary

Here is a summary and reference section for any students or teachers who would like to have a concise review of common punctuation rules. Keep in mind that punctuation requires a knowledge of all four levels of grammar.

A note of caution: even though it is important for the student writer to learn and apply standard and sensible rules of punctuation, it is also important to realize that any strict set of rules is partly subjective and arbitrary; great writers you read will frequently violate—usually for artistic reasons—any set of rules of punctuation or grammar that we might formulate. Hemingway, for example, made an art form out of the run-on sentence. But notice that if you did not know what the standard punctuation was, you would be blind to the creative artistic maneuvering of the great writer.

In addition, punctuation preferences and standards vary. Some style manuals would have you omit the final comma before the coordinating conjunction in a list, whereas others, such as Strunk and White's *Elements of Style*, would ask you to retain it. You will also see differing preferences about the proper construction of dashes, which can be made like this - like this--like this -- or even like this—depending partly on whether you are using a typewriter or computer. In the end, you try to pick sensible principles for punctuating—principles that bring order to your ideas. The principles of punctuation I prefer are given below, for you to use or adapt. They are the principles upon which the punctuation tests in this text are based.

In thinking about the importance of punctuation, it is useful to remember the words of Oscar Wilde, when asked what he had done today, he said:

I spent the whole morning

putting in a comma,

and the whole afternoon

taking it out.

## comma: ( , )

**after introductory participle phrases:** Falling quickly, he sang.

**after introductory interjections:** Yes, I do.

**after informal salutations:** Dear Dante,

**after long introductory prepositional phrases:**

In the chill early morning wind, we moved forward.

**after multiple introductory prepositional phrases:**

At the beginning of the competition, she learned anxiety.

**after introductory dependent clauses (D,I):** If you go, I go.

**after the day and year:** January 3, 1987, was cold.

**after the city and state:** Florence, Italy, is windy.

**around nonessential (nonrestrictive) clauses:**

The dog, which had a nice smile, turned back.

**around nonessential participle phrases:**

My friend, laughing with delight, produced the chicken.

**around most appositives:** Hamlet, my good friend, is visiting.

**around nouns of direct address:** Yes, Hamlet, I will.

**around parenthetical expressions:** I always, bless me, sneeze.

**before coordinating conjunctions in I,ccI compound sentences:**

I have some mutton, and he has some jerky.

**between all items in a list:** tall, dark, handsome, and smart

**between adjectives preceding a noun:** A smart, friendly man

**between contrasts introduced by** *not*: It's here, not there.

**between name and degree or title:** Marcus Aurelius, Ph.D.

**inside closing quotation marks:** "Shut up," he explained.

**NOT after a short prepositional phrase:** In May we departed.

**NOT between compound subjects/predicates:** Hamlet and Ophelia do.

**NOT between subject and verb:** Wrong: My good friend, is here.

## semicolon: ( ; )

**between independent clauses if no coordinating conjunction: I;I**

I am an expert; he is a neophyte.

**between items in a list if the items themselves contain commas:**

We ordered bacon; fried, scrambled, and poached eggs; and grits.

**between independent clauses joined by** ***however*****,** etc.

We all wanted to go; however, only Ishmael departed.

## colon: ( : )

**before a list that is not a compound direct object or subject complement:**

There are three categories: wishes, lies, and dreams.

**before a long formal statement:** To whom it may concern:

**before a long quotation, as in a research paper.**

**between hours and minutes in time:** 6:15
**between Bible chapter and verse:** Luke 4:16
**after formal salutations:** Dear Sir:
**between titles and subtitles:** *Walt Whitman: Poet of America*

## italics: (*no* or no) (italics and underlining are understood to be the same thing)

**title of a book:** A Tale of Two Cities *Treasure Island*
**title of a magazine:** *Life* National Geographic
**title of a work of art:** Mona Lisa *David*
**title of a train or airplane:** Spirit of St. Louis *The Hindenburg*
**words, letters, and numbers as such:** the word *blubber*, the letter *a*, the number *5*
**foreign language words:** *dejà vu*

**Underline (use italics) when you are referring to a word itself**. Words, numbers, and letters *as such* must be placed in italics, which means—on a typewriter—that they must be underlined (NOT put in quotation marks!). In this way we distinguish the word *dog* from the animal, dog. We use *b*'s in spelling, and we use *3*'s in counting. See? We also place foreign language words in italics/underline: Homer begins his story *in medias res*, in the middle of things. This technique will be especially important when you are analyzing poetry or literature and are making reference to the words, letters, or sounds contained in the writing.

**Underline titles.** The titles of books, newspapers, ships, trains, works of art, major musical compositions, and other important titles are always to be placed in italics, both in the body of a research paper and in the Works Cited. If you are typing, this means that you underline the title, though in a published document *italics is the style in which the letters lean to the right*. In other words, when you see a title in a book, the title will look like this: *A Midsummer Night's Dream,* but in a research paper it will look like this: A Midsummer Night's Dream. Titles should **not** be placed in quotation marks or in upper case in lieu of italics. Less significant titles, such as the titles of chapters, articles, poems, or songs, do not deserve italics; these titles are only placed in quotation marks. In a Works Cited listing, book titles are only to be underlined; they are not also enclosed in quotation marks.

## quotation marks: ( " " )

**around a direct quotation:** He said, "I am not a crook."
**commas and periods go inside quotes:** "Chocolate," he said.
**colons and semicolons go outside quotes:** He said, "Hi"; I left.
**title of short story, poem, song:** "The Road Not Taken"
**title of article, chapter, or part of publication:**
The fourth chapter of My False Demise is entitled "Rumors."
**NOT to indicate cute, trite, or ungrammatical terms:**
Hi, "Buddies," how about a "pep talk!"

## **apostrophe**: ( ' )

**noun made into a possessive adjective:** John's boat
**missing letter in a contraction:** don't
**missing number in a year contraction:** '47
**plurals of letters, numbers, signs, and words as such:** a's 5's
**with an** *s* to show possession after a singular noun: Dickens's
**alone to show possession after a plural noun ending in** *s*: dogs'
**for quotations within quotations:**
John said, "Hamlet cried, 'Oops!' when he fell."
**in the contraction of *it* and *is*:** it's
**NOT in the possessive pronoun *its*.**
**NOT in plural centuries or decades:** 1900s the 50s

## **hyphen**: ( - )

**word divided at end of line**
**compound written numbers from** twenty-one to ninety-nine
**fractions used as adjectives:** a three-fourths majority
**prefixes before proper noun or proper adjective:** Pre-Raphaelite
**compound nouns that include prepositional phrases:** father-in-law
**compound adjective when it** *precedes* its noun: a well-meant lie
**NOT in compound adjectives** *after* nouns: It was well meant.
**do NOT use a hyphen (-) when you intend a dash (-- or —)**

## **dash**: (-- or —)

**abrupt break in thought:** So I--wait a minute!--ate the fish.
**to show omitted words in dialogue:**
He said, "Come here, you young . . . ."
**To make a dash on a typewriter type two hyphens with NO spaces--like that.**
**NOT to replace proper punctuation.**

## **ellipsis**: ( . . . )

**to indicate words omitted from quotations**
**Use three periods if the omission is within a sentence.**
**Use four periods if the omission includes sentence ending.**
**Type blank spaces between the periods of an ellipsis . . . see?**

The ellipsis, an elaboration: This comment must be in Courier font. Learn to use and properly construct the ellipsis. We use an ellipsis, a series of spaces and periods, to indicate that we have left out part of a quotation. If you are only quoting a phrase, you need no ellipsis at all: We saw by the "dawn's early light." We need not begin a short quote with an ellipsis if a lower-case letter clearly indicates that the first word quoted was not the first word of the sentence: Fitzgerald replied that he "needed no instructions from Hemingway." We do begin a long quote with a three-period ellipsis if we have left out the beginning of the sentence. A simple omission within a sentence requires a three-period ellipsis with spaces before and after every period: "But as for me . . . give me death." If you are omitting the end of a question, you put the question mark after the ellipsis: We would ask "How many angels can dance . . . ?" Finally, if we are omitting the final word or words of a sentence (or more than one sentence), we must include a fourth period--the one to end the sentence: "Mary had a little lamb. . . . And everywhere that Mary went the lamb was sure to go." Notice the spacing; the extra period occurs immediately after the final quoted word, with no intervening space. If you are using documentary notes (as we do in our research papers) and you stop quoting right after the ellipsis, then you put the extra period AFTER the documentary note: As Mother Goose has noted, "Mary had a little lamb. Its fleece was white . . ." (Goose 472).

## **parenthesis**: ( ( ) )

**around parenthetical remarks added to a sentence:**

He said I would be (I wish!) six feet tall.

## **brackets**: ( [ ] )

**around words inserted into quoted material:**

Johnson notes, "At this time [Dickens] began to weaken."

When you insert words into quotations--usually for the purpose of clarifying references or enhancing the flow of the sentences--you must enclose your inserted words in brackets like [this] to show that these words were not part of the original quote. Be sure to use [brackets] rather than (parentheses) or <mathematical symbols>. Computer word processors usually have brackets, but what if you are using a typewriter? Sometimes people carefully add brackets with a pen after the paper is typed, since most typewriters do not have brackets, but you can also make your own brackets on a typewriter by using a combination of underlines and slants:

slants and underlines /make the brackets/ like that.

**question mark**: ( **?** )

**at the end of an interrogative sentence:** Do you have dogs?
**inside closing quotes if part of quote:** He asked, "Is there time?"
**outside quotes if not part of quote:** Did he say, "Remember me"?

**period**: ( **.** )

**at the end of a declarative sentence:** I have three dogs.
**at the end of a mild imperative sentence:** Please go away.
**after most abbreviations:** Dr. Trelawney
**inside closing quotation marks:** He said, "Go away."

**exclamation point**: ( **!** )

**after an exclamatory sentence:** The sky is falling!
**after a strong imperative sentence:** Get out!
**NOT to express chronic cuteness:** Hi! Guess what!!

**virgule or slash ( / )**

When you are quoting poetry in a research paper, you don't have to return to a new line just because you reach the end of a line of the poem. Instead of returning to a new line, you may—if you wish—just insert a slash ( / ) at the point where the poem drops to a new line. Include one space before and after the slash: Mary had a little lamb, / Its fleece was white as snow, / And every where that Mary went / The lamb was sure to go. The slash will separate the lines of poetry for the reader. Of course, you can quote the lines in a column as they appear in the book also.

In other words, if you see this in a book:

> Mary had a little lamb,
> Its fleece was white as snow,
> And every where that Mary went
> The lamb was sure to go.

You can type it this way in your paper if you want to:

> Mary had a little lamb, / Its fleece was white as snow, / And every where that Mary went / The lamb was sure to go.

**space**: ( or )

**Type one space between words.**
Type one space after a comma.
**Type two spaces after the closing punctuation in each sentence:**

```
Do it like this.  Not like this. See?
```

**Indent** *five* spaces for a new paragraph.
**Indent** *ten* spaces for a long quotation.
**Leave a space between periods in an ellipsis: . . . not: ...**
Leave NO spaces on either side of a dash or hyphen: pro-McGovern.
Do *not* use only one single space between sentences.

## Just give me some **Space**:

Spaces: This section of The Magic Lens must again be in Courier type font, ragged right, in order to illustrate spacing matters that occur in research papers:

Always place two blank spaces after the period or other closing punctuation at the end of a sentence.  We insert two blank spaces after all of the periods within each of the Works Cited listings.  Place only a single blank space between two words in a sentence.  Be sure to leave one blank space after commas, like that.  If you don't,see what happens.  The same rule applies to colons: leave one space afterwards; you also leave one blank space after semicolons, not two. You should leave a blank space after numbers followed by closing parentheses, 1) like that, rather than 2)like that.  You do not leave a space before the punctuation , only after it.

When you type a three-period ellipsis, use four spaces to separate the three periods, like . . . this, rather than putting the periods together like...this. You should not leave blank spaces just inside quotation marks, parentheses, or brackets; these marks should be closed up against the words they enclose, (like this) rather than ( like this ).  After an abbreviation's period, you use a single blank space: you would type "Mr. Dickens," not "Mr.  Dickens."  In parenthetical notes, leave a single space between the closing quotes and the parenthetical note "that follows, like this" (Jones 54).  Leave two blank spaces between the period and the documentary note at the end of a long quotation.

Again: Do **not** put blank spaces inside quotation marks " like this " or within parentheses ( like this ); quotes and parentheses should be closed up around the words they enclose "like" (this).

I think of the blank space almost as one of the letters--it is the null letter, the act of placing a blank in the space. The blank space is a language object just as a letter or punctuation mark is a language object. The blank space has meaning; changes in spacing can cause changes in interpretation. Again: We normally put a single space between words in a sentence, a single space after colons and semicolons, a single space between Mr. and Name, and two blank spaces after the closing punctuation of each sentence.

# Common English Grammar and Usage Problems

The following collection of common grammar errors and usage problems may be used as a general reference and as a reference for the Solecism Theater projects.

To **accept** is to take: I can accept no money for this harpoon.
To **except** is to omit: I can except no one from the rule except you.

To **affect** is to influence: Your idea will affect many people.
The verb **effect** means cause: Your idea will effect a new procedure.
The noun **effect** means result: Your idea will produce a good effect.

Use **afraid of** and **frightened by**, rather than **frightened of**: Ahab had been frightened by a whale, and was afraid of them ever since.

To **aggravate** is to make worse, not to irritate: It irritated me that she went out in the rain and aggravated her cold.

Use **all right**, not **alright**: We will be all right if the Spartans arrive.

An **allusion** is a reference: His comment was an allusion to the *Iliad*.
An **illusion** is a deception: The bas relief gave the illusion of depth.

In ordinary sentences, do not substitute the **ampersand (&)** or the mathematical **plus symbol (+)** for the coordinating conjunction **and**.

**Bad** is an adjective: The bad decision ruined the project.
**Badly** is an adverb: The bad swimmer did not swim badly.

The reason is not **because**; the reason is **that**: The reason we think carefully is that we regret our errors.

Something is **between** two: This secret is between you and me.
Something is **among** three or more: Divide the fish among the five dogs.

We **bring** toward, but we **take** away: If you take someone's lunch by mistake, you must bring it back to him or her.

**Can** means able to: You can repair a door if you know how.
**May** means are permitted to: Yes, you may leave the room.

Not **could of** or **should of**, but **could have** or **should have**: I could have read classics, and I should have read classics.
(We sometimes see **could've** as the contraction of **could have** and **should've** as the contraction of **should have**.)

**Disinterested** means without prejudice because of having no personal interest in something: We need a disinterested judge to try this case fairly. **Uninterested** means without interest in the sense of being bored: The boy was uninterested in the story, and began to daydream. A disinterested judge could find a case very interesting.

Use **done** only with a helping verb: I have done nothing to you.

**Don't** is the contraction of "do not": We don't like egocentrism.
**Doesn't** is the contraction of "does not": He doesn't like ethnocentrism.
**Don't** use **don't** for singular subjects: He don't like eggplant.

To **emigrate** is to migrate out: The family emigrated from Russia.
To **immigrate** is to migrate in: The family immigrated to Puerto Rico.

Use **farther** for distance: Her javelin went farther than his did.
Use **further** for time: We will consider this matter further.

Use **feel bad** rather than **feel badly**.

Use **fewer** for countable things: There are fewer players.
Use **less** for uncountable amount: There is less sugar.

If you are enumerating elements in your essay, use **first** and **second**, rather than **firstly** and **secondly**. The latter terms with their **-ly** suffix have a supercilious, pedantic ring to them that is undesirable. In fact, Thomas Hardy even satirized the use of such language in one of his poems, "Channel Firing." In the poem, a skeleton wakes up in the grave and muses satirically about someone he knows, "Parson Thirdly."

**Fortuitous** means by chance: A fortuitous circumstance occurred.
**Fortunate** means lucky: A fortunate condition resulted.

**Good** is an adjective: The good swimmer swam her fastest time.
**Well** is usually an adverb: The good swimmer swam well.
**Well** can sometimes be an adjective: He is not a well man.

Clothes, when put out to dry, are **hung**. People, when strung up to die, are **hanged**. Oedipus enters the palace to find that Jocasta has hanged herself.

**Hopefully** is an adverb meaning "full of hope"; it should not be used as a substitute for **I hope**: I hope that you will strive hopefully for knowledge.

Note the difference between **ideas** and **ideals**. **Ideas** are concepts, thoughts, and so forth. We could discuss the philosophical ideas of Friedrich Nietzsche. **Ideals** are standards, goals to be attained, ideas of excellence or perfection. Both ideas and ideals are mental, but we debate ideas while striving for the ideal.

It is best to use the word **impact** only as a noun, and not as a verb, in discussing the effect of individuals on history. When we say that x "impacted" y, this usage has an unfortunate, unpleasant medical connotation that is undesirable. The preferable word is **affected**. We affect others, rather than impact them, and when we affect them, this has an impact.

To **imply** is to suggest: He implied that we were to blame.
To **infer** is to deduce: We inferred that we were being blamed.

**It's** is the contraction of **it is**: It's fun to understand things.
**its** is a possessive pronoun: The alien chomped its jaws.

Use **kind of** rather than **kind of a**: It seemed to be some kind of nose.

Use **lend** as a verb: Lend me money for a harpoon.
Use **loan** as a noun: Give me a loan for a harpoon.

To **lie** (v.i.) is to rest: I will lie here in the shade.
To **lay** (v.t.) is to put: I will lay the book here on the rock.

Use **like** as a preposition: We have good books like these.
Use **as** as a conjunction: We have good books, as you have.

**Literally** means actually, not figuratively. You could say, "We literally left within two minutes," but you could not say, "We literally vanished." If you did not physically vanish, then you did not literally vanish.

In the past we used the terms **man** and **mankind**, and even the possessive pronoun **his**, to refer to all human beings, both male and female. Today, our sensitivities have improved, and we try to avoid defaulting to the masculine gender when we intend to express something which also includes women. Other terms, such as **human beings**, **humanity**, **persons**, and even the compound pronouns such as **his or her** sound more accurate and more fair.

**Myself** and **yourself** should be used as reflexive or intensive pronouns rather than as direct objects. "I, myself, believed it" is correct usage, but "She asked John and myself if we had the loot" is not. It would be correct to say, "She asked John and me if we had the loot."

**Nauseous** means sickening: It was a nauseous sight.
**Nauseated** means sick at the stomach: I was nauseated by the sight.

**Number** is for countables: There were a number of soldiers there.
**Amount** is for uncountables: There was an enormous amount of tension.

Use **off** rather than **off of**: The ball bounced off the backboard.

**Phenomenon** is singular and **phenomena** is plural: The most interesting phenomenon of all the meteorological phenomena was the tornado.

Save **plus** for mathematics and use **in addition to** in most other situations: They wanted burgers. In addition to that, they wanted shakes.

**Precipitate** means hasty, and **precipitous** means steep: He made a precipitate decision to descend the precipitous path.

The phrase **relate to** is a vague colloquialism. Instead of saying that many people *relate to* J.D. Salinger's character Holden Caulfield, say that many people *understand* Holden, or that they find that Holden's struggles remind them of their own struggles, or something specific. To say we *relate to* Holden is vague. In what way do we relate? Do we feel the same alienation from conventional society that he feels? Do we have dreams similar to his dream of being the catcher in the rye? Do we love our little brothers and sisters? Do we feel that his language expresses our own view of the world? Do we feel ourselves losing our emotional our psychological health? There are so many thousands of relationships that simply to say one thing relates to another is almost to communicate nothing at all; you have to use a specific word that names that specific relationship.

Use **raise** transitively: They will attempt to raise the Titanic.
Use **rise** intransitively: She began to rise slowly through the air.

Use **regardless** rather than **irregardless**.

**Respectfully** is with respect: He spoke respectfully of his father.
**Respectively** is in sequence: He spoke of his father, his brother, and his sister, respectively.

Use **since** rather than **seeing as how**: Since you feel that way, I will do the work myself.

You **sit** (v.i.) down in a chair: She was sitting there on the porch.

You **set** (v.t.) down a book: She was setting the book on the step.

**Someone** is not they. Rather than saying, "Someone dropped their headphones," say, "Someone dropped a pair of headphones." Use **they** or **their** when you intend to refer to a group of people.

You **teach** people things, and you **learn** subjects: you do not learn people things: If you would like to learn algebra, I can teach you.

**Than** is a conjunction: We have more perplexities than you have.
**Then** is an adverb: We will go now; you go then.

**Them** should be used as an object pronoun, not as an adjective: And so, my friends, ask not when you can have them cookies, ask when you can have those cookies.

**They're** is the contraction of "they are": They're reading now.
**Their** is a possessive pronoun: They're reading their books.
**There** is a place: They're reading their books there.

Use **this** rather than **this here**: This dog bit me on this foot.

**To** is a preposition or an infinitive: She went to Boston to think.
**Too** is an adverb meaning "also" or "too much": I sleep too much, too.
**Two** is a number: Two twins twisted twine in the twilight.

**Tortuous** means full of twists: a tortuous highway.
**Torturous** means full of torture: a torturous ordeal.

Use **try to** rather than **try and**: Please try to help today.

Something is either **unique**, one of a kind, or it is not. There are no degrees of uniqueness, and so nothing can be **very** unique.

Use **way off** rather than **ways off**: He was a long way off.

**Who** is a subject pronoun: Who is here?
**Whom** is an object pronoun: To whom do you wish to speak?

**Who** refers to people: It was they who followed the truck.
**That** and **which** refer to objects: Which rock is that?

**Who's** is the contraction of **who** and **is**. Who's going to think?
**Whose** is a pronoun or adjective: Whose woods these are, I think I know.

# Solecism Theater

## (A Usage Mastery Project)

### Student Instructions

**Solecism Theater**: In ancient Cilicia in the city of Soloi, the citizens spoke a corrupt form of Attic Greek, regarded by the Athenians as crude, foolish, and ungrammatical. This feeling of distaste for the Soloi-cisms spoken in Soloi has given us our word **solecism** (soh-leh-sism), which means a blunder in language, an ungrammatical usage, a misuse of language. **Solecism Theater** is a creative play-writing usage project in which students write short (3-5 minute) humorous plays which derive their humor from the contradictions and confusions of language usage errors.

**Instructions**: For one of the following three situations (or for one which you create), write a funny play of three to five minutes, which dramatically and vividly illustrates the difference between standard English usage and solecism. This is not a solemn scholarly assignment: make your play original, witty, or satirical. Have fun. Notice that titles are not provided for any of the play situations; you must write a creative title for your play.

**Here's the catch**: *Every sentence* must illustrate either correct usage or incorrect usage. Try to include a variety of different common usage errors in your play, and try to show the same usage in both correct and incorrect forms. Note that some misunderstandings (*they're*, *their*, *there*) become most noticeable in written language, so if you include them, you will need to creatively write your play so that the audience will understand what is happening when the play is performed.

**Open Book**: Solecism Theater is not a test of your usage knowledge. In writing your solecism play, you may use the usage discussion in this text as an open-book reference, or you may use other published usage discussions if your teacher allows.

**Performance**: After you write your play, you will be given an opportunity to perform it in class. You may need to have other students help you perform your play. Feel free to incorporate clever props and costumes.

## Someone Dropped Their Banana:
A Sample Solecism Play
MC Thompson

Fred and Joe enter. Fred looks down, and picks up a banana.

Fred: Look, someone dropped their banana.
Joe: How did you know many people own that banana?
Fred: Hopefully, they don't!
Joe: It makes those people feel *hopeful* to not own the banana?
Fred: Are you trying to aggravate me?
Joe: No, I'm not trying to make you worse; you said it was "their banana," I just want to know who they are, and why they're so hopeful about their banana.
Fred: I ain't never said they were hopeful about no banana.
Joe: Oh, so you admit you said it.
Fred: I ain't never said it.
Joe: Let me get this straight: You said the people don't own a banana hopefully.
Fred: I'll not discuss this farther. I said someone dropped their banana.
Joe: You won't discuss this farther?
Fred: Right.
Joe: Then how close do you want me to stand, so we can talk about it?
Fred: I want you to stand a-ways over there, and leave me alone.
Joe: But you said you didn't want to discuss it farther.
Fred: I ain't gonna discuss it no farther.
Joe: Then why are you sending me farther?
Fred: You're trying to aggravate me, for sure.
Joe: No, I'm just trying to improve you.
Fred: Now, what're you inferring?
Joe: I can't infer anything, you have me confused.
Fred: If you ask me, you are literally a bird.
Joe: I am a mammal.
Fred: I see I can't learn you nothing.
Joe: What do you want to learn about me?
Fred: Your nonsense is making me feel nauseous.
Joe: No, I think you look fine.
Fred: I didn't say nothing about how I look!
Joe: You said you made me sick.
Fred: I didn't never say that.
Joe: That's right, you did.
Fred: See here, even with a lot of dark, rotten places, I'm gonna eat this banana.
Joe: I didn't realize you were sick. What disease do you have?
Fred: I ain't got no disease!
Joe: I'm so sorry to hear it. Where do you have these dark, rotten places, on your stomach? Let me see.
Fred: I never said I had no dark, rotten place, I said there were rotten places on the banana.
Joe: You mean you got a skin disease from a banana?
Fred: This conversation is literally splitting my head.
Joe: Oh, no! Now I understand why you said you were nauseous.

Fred runs away screaming, and Joe sits down, peels the banana, and eats it.

Write a 3-5 minute Solecism Play based on one of the following situations or on one which you create. Remember to write a creative title for your play.

**Situation 1**: Two individuals meet on the street. One can utter no correct sentence, and the other can utter no incorrect sentence. Their humorous interchange revolves around one person trying to correct the other's spoken grammar, but the latter is so used to hearing incorrect grammar, that he doesn't realize he's being corrected, and keeps missing the point that it's his own language which is at issue.

**Situation 2**: Two individuals are surreptitiously whispering and writing notes in a class as the teacher is lecturing on problems of English usage. Neither student is paying any attention to the lecture, and both are holding up their notes for the other to see. The two students each have serious spoken and written usage problems. The juxtaposition of the students' usage errors with the teacher's lecture on those very problems makes an amusing and ironic story.

**Situation 3**: Two friends meet by surprise. One can speak no sentence without a pronoun error (of agreement, or case, or reference), and the other can speak no sentence without a subject/verb disagreement. Provide your own topic for their conversation.

**Situation 4**: On a distant planet in 2071, a citizen in the American colony goes out to eat at a fast food joint, where only the latest crazes in colonial fast foods are served. The person taking fast food orders can ask no question which is free of usage errors, and the citizen tries to answer the questions correctly, but the food order is incredibly fouled up as a result of the exasperating language problem. No matter how hard the order taker and the citizen try to communicate, things only become worse.

**Situation 5**: Two friends write to each other. One friend writes a one-page letter in which no sentence is without a usage problem. The letter contains a wide variety of different usage problems and common punctuation errors, some of which are also problems of spoken language. The second friend writes back, discussing the same matters in correct usage.

**Situation 6**: In the presence of a group of people, two individuals have a misunderstanding caused by a classic pronoun reference error: one of the two makes the "adolescent *they*" error in every single sentence, and the second always thinks that *they* or *their* refers to the group of people nearby, which causes a major misunderstanding to develop!

# Loops

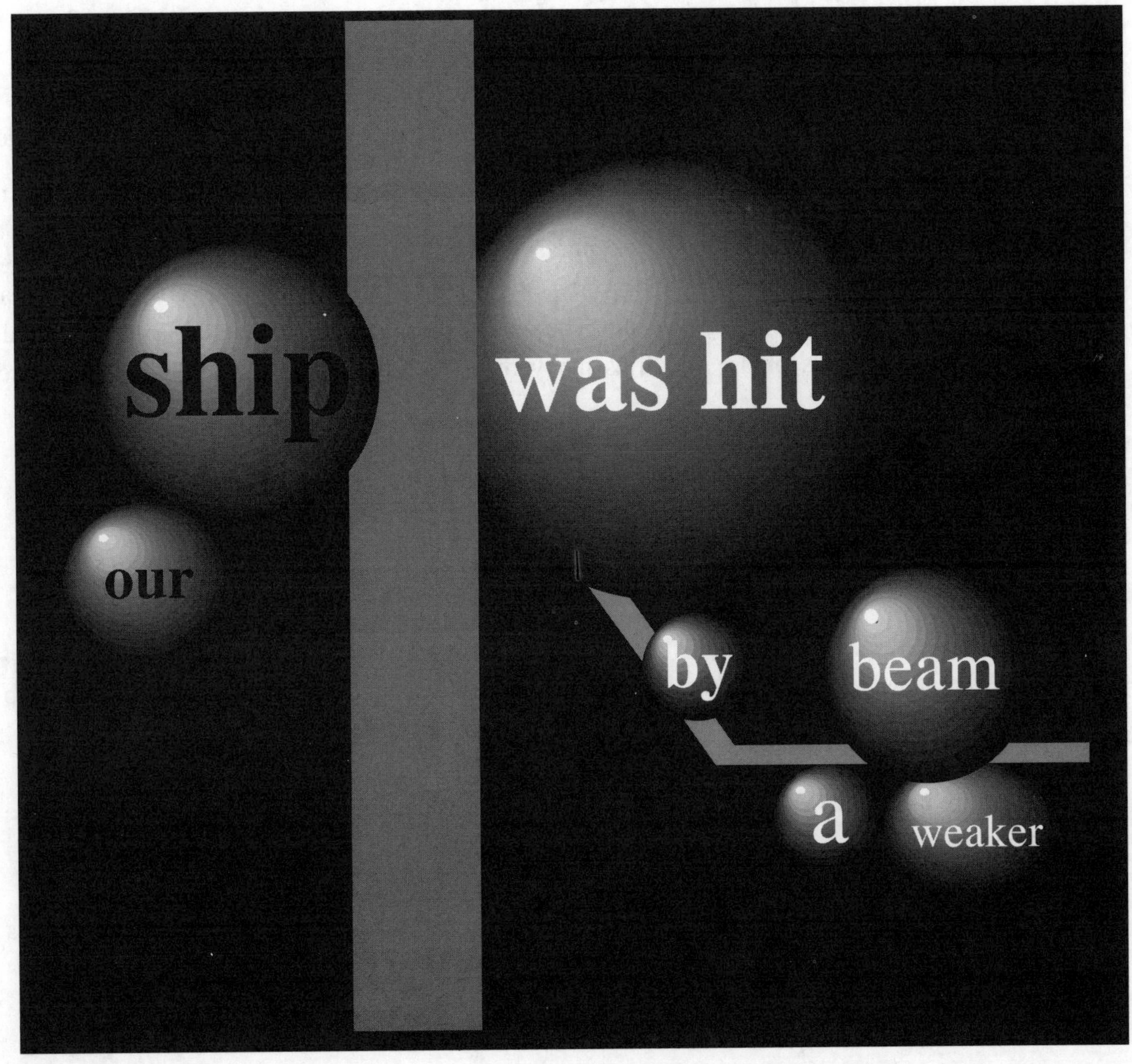

## The Martian visitors will have landed by Thursday.

**Parts of speech**: *The* is an adjective (definite article) modifying the plural common noun *visitors*; *Martian* is a proper adjective that also modifies *visitors*; *will* and *have* are helping verbs that help the main verb *landed* form the future perfect tense; *by* is a preposition, and *Thursday* is a proper noun that is also the object of the preposition *by*.

**Parts of the sentence**: The subject is *visitors*, and *will have landed* is the verb/simple predicate.

**Phrases**: The sentence contains two phrases. The first is a verb phrase, *will have landed*, that consists of a main verb and two helping verbs. We often show the tense of a verb by creating a phrase: *will fly, has flown, will have flown*, etc. The second phrase in this sentence is a prepositional phrase, *by Thursday*. This phrase modifies the verb. Remember that prepositional phrases are always modifiers.

**Clauses**: This is a simple, declarative sentence based on a single subject and predicate. It is simple because it contains one clause, and it is declarative because it makes a statement.

• • •

Perfect tense: Remember that the perfect tenses are called *perfect* after the Latin verb *perficere*, to finish. If I *will have landed* by Thursday, I *will have finished* by then.

Proper adjective: *Martian* is a proper adjective, capitalized because it derives from the proper noun, *Mars*.

Remember: There is a Four-Level Analysis sentence at the beginning of each loop, and it is these very sentences that are used in the Grammar Review Test. Be sure to study these sentences carefully.

## FOUR-LEVEL ANALYSIS

| | The | Martian | visitors | will | have | landed | by | Thursday. |
|---|---|---|---|---|---|---|---|---|
| **Parts of Speech:** | adj. | adj. | n. | v. | v. | v. | prep. | n. |
| **Parts of Sentence:** | | | subject | ------predicate----- | | | | |
| **Phrases:** | | | | | | | --prep. phrase-- | |
| **Clauses:** | one independent clause, simple declarative sentence | | | | | | | |

This sentence illustrates the logic of prepositional phrase modification. We know that prepositional phrases are modifiers, so every prepositional phrase is either an adjective or an adverb. Which one is this? One way to tell is to remember the preposition placement rule: any prepositional phrase that modifies a noun must be place immediately after it. So *by Thursday* can not modify *visitors*, it can only modify the verb. By this same rule the phrase would modify the verb if the phrase came at the beginning of the sentence.

## BINARY DIAGRAM

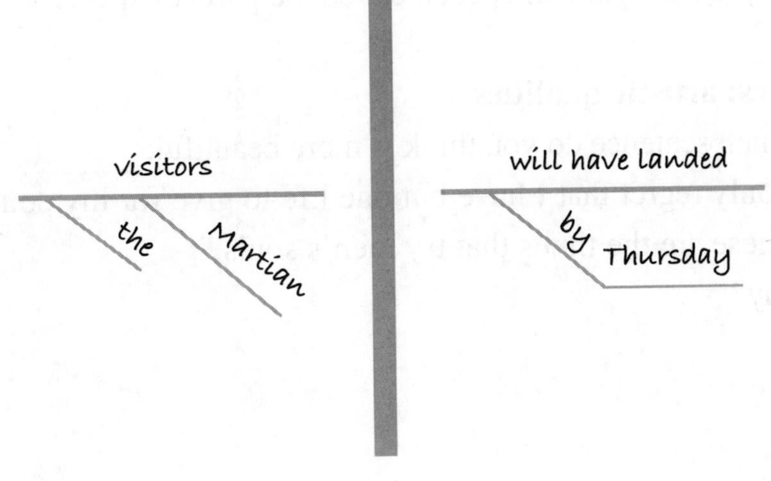

**Questions for individual thought or small group discussion:**

**synthesis: making connections**

You look up a verb in the dictionary and find that, in addition to a definition, the dictionary entry contains the letters *v.t.* in italics. What does that tell you about how that verb is to be used? How many forms of knowledge have to come together in your brain to enable you to look up and comprehend the abbreviation *v.t.*?

**divergence: thinking of alternatives**

Grammar is a way of thinking about language, but another way of saying that is that *grammar helps you to organize ideas.* Think of as many ways as you can in which grammar helps you to organize ideas, and consider this question one level at a time, beginning with parts of speech, then parts of the sentence, then phrases, and then clauses.

**analysis: breaking down into components**

Why are the parts of speech called the parts of speech?

**aesthetics: artistic qualities**

Which sentence do you think is more beautiful:
"I only regret that I have but one life to give for my country."
"These are the times that try men's souls."
Why?

Use the grammar clues to solve this Mystery Sentence:

A children's story contains a compound declarative sentence distinguished by three independent clauses. A coordinating conjunction is used twice to join the three clauses together. Each clause contains a contraction of the first person singular subject pronoun and the helping verb *will*. The third clause contains a second person singular possessive adjective, a direct object, and an adverb. The first two clauses contain only subjects and verbs. What is the sentence?

From Nathaniel Hawthorne's

# *The Scarlet Letter*

A throng of bearded men, in sad-colored garments and gray, steeple-crowned hats, intermixed with women, some wearing hoods, and others bareheaded, was assembled in front of a wooden edifice, the door of which was heavily timbered with oak and studded with iron spikes.

What is the style of this first paragraph from Nathaniel Hawthorne's classic? How many sentences are in the paragraph? How many words in the sentence? Is there a direct object? What is the subject/predicate set? How many adjectives are in the paragraph? What generalizations could you make about the style of the paragraph? What do you notice about, and how can you explain, the following consonants:

A throng of bearded men, in sad-colored garments and gray, steeple-crowned hats, intermixed with women, some wearing hoods, and others bareheaded, was assembled in front of a wooden edifice, the door of which was heavily timbered with oak and studded with iron spikes.

1. Write a simple declarative sentence that has a compound subject consisting of one common noun and one proper noun, that has a verb consisting of a main verb and a helping verb, that contains a direct object, and that contains an indefinite article.

2. Write a complex declarative sentence that contains a dependent clause beginning with a subordinating conjunction followed by an independent clause which includes a subject complement.

# Loop One Writing Lab
# Prepositional Phrases

1. Describe a peaceful woodland scene, with an animal moving through or across it. You can choose any animal you like. The description should be between fifty and a hundred words long.

2. After you finish, read your paragraph, then go back and strike through the prepositional phrases.

3. See if you can think of a different way to include the information that used to be in the prepositional phrases.

4. Write your own definition of *preposition* and *prepositional phrase*.

## "O, what a rogue and peasant slave am I."

## -William Shakespeare

Perhaps Shakespeare's greatest play, *Hamlet,* contains this classic line of self-doubt, when Hamlet cries in soliloquy: "Oh, what a rogue and peasant slave am I!" Analyze the four levels of grammar in Hamlet's sentence.

**Parts of speech**: *Oh* is an interjection; *what* is an adjective modifying the noun *rogue*; the indefinite article *a* is also an adjective modifying *rogue*; *and* is a coordinating conjunction joining the nouns *rogue* and *slave* into a compound; *peasant* is here used as an adjective to modify the noun *slave*; *am* is a present tense linking verb*; I* is a first person singular subject pronoun.

**Parts of the sentence**: The subject of this sentence is *I*; its predicate is the linking verb *am*: the linking verb connects the subject to a compound subject complement, the two nouns *rogue* and slave; which are predicate nominatives. The sentence is notable for its effective inversion, putting the despised subject of Hamlet's sentence, himself, last, to echo in the silence of the period.

**Phrases**: There are no prepositional, appositive, or verbal phrases.

**Clauses**: This is a simple declarative sentence, consisting of only one clause, since it has only one subject/predicate set.

### FOUR-LEVEL ANALYSIS

| | **Oh,** | **what** | **a** | **rogue** | **and** | **peasant** | **slave** | **am** | **I.** |
|---|---|---|---|---|---|---|---|---|---|
| **Parts of Speech:** | interj. | adj. | adj. | n. | conj. | adj. | n. | v. | pron. |
| **Parts of Sentence:** | | | | ---- compound subject complement---- | | | | pred. | subj. |
| **Phrases:** | | | | -------------no phrase-------------- | | | | | |
| **Clauses:** | | one independent clause, simple declarative sentence | | | | | | | |

For the next ten sentences, identify the **part of speech** of the word in **bold**:

1. Do **bacilli** and fungi have nuclei in their cells? ______________
2. Can a system of justice **ever** be unjust? ______________
3. The **luminous** moonlight illuminated the *Pequod*. ______________
4. The **superannuated** doorman celebrated his fiftieth anniversary. ______________
5. At the satellite's **apogee** we could not find it with binoculars. ______________
6. The senior class president **befriended** the venerable man. ______________
7. **On** his solo transcontinental flight, he enjoyed the solitude. ______________
8. Basic instructions are **included** with each new bassoon. ______________
9. The interrogation was **derogatory** in tone. ______________
10. Several members of **Parliament** had a parley in the parlor. ______________

For the next ten sentences, identify the **part of sentence** of the word in **bold**:

11. The **plenipotentiary** met twice with the potentate. ______________
12. The surge of the sea portended the **resurgence** of violence. ______________
13. The philologist delighted in inventing witty **neologisms**. ______________
14. The grammar in the telegram was not **correct**. ______________
15. During the holy man's incantation, the spirit began **to appear**. ______________
16. There **were** no regal ceremonies in the interregnum. ______________
17. The doctor's prognosis gave **Diogenes** renewed hope. ______________
18. The musician's androgynous **appearance** was widely imitated. ______________
19. The secret agent spilled the deadly chemical **agent**. ______________
20. There may be little **time** to act or react. ______________

For the next ten sentences, identify the phrase in **bold**:

1. Bulgakov, **the anarchist's friend**, had a severe case of anemia. ______________
2. **Complaining loudly**, the absentee landlord was abruptly abducted ______________
3. We advised the adventurer **to admire his adversary**. ______________
4. The melodeon played a sappy melody **during the melodrama**. ______________
5. The pilot tried **to study aeronautics and aerodynamics**. ______________
6. The albino stared **at the white pages** of the blank album. ______________
7. Luciferase is the enzyme **in the luminous organs** of the firefly. ______________
8. Does Franklin's epitaph contain a witty epigram **for posterity**? ______________
9. **At the exhumation**, the rich humus was removed. ______________
10. **Viewing microbes** is a favorite habit of biologists. ______________

For the next ten sentences, identify the sentence structure (disregard bold type).

11. The bonny lass discovered the **bonanza** by accident. ______________
12. We learned, and the **superstructure** was constructed in three days. ______________
13. They left when chlorine damaged the **chlorophyll** in the plants. ______________
14. He held the **cyanotype** to the light and she admired the blue lines. ______________
15. The **cytologist** watched the leucocytes and erythrocytes. ______________
16. She folded the **diploma** and handed it to the waiting diplomat. ______________
17. His **dyslexia** made it hard to pronounce words, but he succeeded. ______________
18. The **ecologist** was fascinated with living things in the ecosystem. ______________
19. The senator had **hypoglycemia**, not anemia, when this occurred. ______________
20. A specialist in dysentery and **enteritis** explained the rare ailment. ______________

For each of the following sentences, circle the letter of each answer that is true. The answer can be any combination, including all or none. This exercise will teach you the real process of punctuation as a function of grammar.

1. In October the Allies advanced and the Axis gathered its resources.

a. a comma after the prepositional phrase
b. a comma after the dependent clause
c. a comma after the independent clause
d. an apostrophe in the contraction
e. commas before and after the appositive

2. In San Antonio Texas the tumbleweed covered Ricardos field.

a. a comma after the city
b. a comma after the state appositive
c. an apostrophe in the plural noun
d. an apostrophe in the possessive noun
e. a comma after the dependent clause

3. A very large moon shone as Alexander the Macedonian conqueror rode forward.

a. a comma between adjectives
b. a comma after the dependent clause
c. a comma after the independent clause
d. commas around the appositive
e. commas around the noun of direct address

4. Hamlet Whitmans book Leaves of Brass is about a train called The Occident Express.

a. italics on the train title
b. an apostrophe in the possessive noun
c. quotation marks around the book title
d. italics on the book title
e. commas around the appositive

5. The well planned party and the serene weather rejuvenated twenty seven friends.

a. comma between adjectives that precede the noun.
b. a hyphen in the compound adjective
c. a comma after the dependent clause
d. a hyphen in the compound number
e. an apostrophe in the possessive noun

## Our ship was hit by a weaker beam.

**Parts of speech**: *Our* is a possessive pronoun modifying the noun *ship*; *ship* is a singular common noun; *was hit* consists of the helping verb *was* and the main verb *hit*; *was hit* is past tense, passive voice action verb; *by* is a preposition; *a* and *weaker* are adjectives modifying the singular common noun *beam*. The adjective *a* is an indefinite article.

**Parts of the sentence**: The subject is *ship*, and the verb is *was hit*. There is no direct object, indirect object, or subject complement.

**Phrases**: The sentence contains a prepositional phrase, *by a weaker beam*. The preposition is *by*, and the object of the preposition is *beam*. The purpose of a prepositional phrase is to modify; this particular prepositional phrase modifies the verb. In other words, this prepositional phrase acts like an adverb, even though the phrase contains no adverb.

**Clauses**: The sentence only contains one clause; it is therefore a simple sentence in structure. The entire sentence is the clause—an independent clause. Within the clause there is a prepositional phrase which is discussed above. Just as the heart can be within the body, so that a person has both a heart and a body, a phrase can be within a clause, so that a sentence can have both a phrase and a clause. In other words, a clause can have a phrase inside it.

• • •

Degrees of adjectives: Some adjectives can be expressed in three degrees. Examples are *good, better, best*; *tall, taller, tallest*; *bad, worse, worst*; and *weak, weaker, weakest*. The names of the three degrees are the **positive** degree (weak), the **comparative** degree (weaker), and the **superlative** degree (weakest). The adjective *weaker* in the sentence above is in the comparative degree.

Active Voice: The sentence above is expressed in passive voice. Often a sentence will have more power if it is reworded to use the active voice. This means that the subject of the sentence will be acting, not acted on. *A weaker beam hit our ship* is the active voice version of the sentence.

## FOUR-LEVEL ANALYSIS

| | Our | ship | was | hit | by | a | weaker | beam. |
|---|---|---|---|---|---|---|---|---|
| **Parts of Speech:** | pron. | n. | v. | v. | prep. | adj. | adj. | n. |
| **Parts of Sentence:** | | subject | --predicate-- | | | | | |
| **Phrases:** | | | | | ----------prepositional phrase--------- | | | |
| **Clauses:** | one independent clause, simple declarative sentence | | | | | | | |

The key concept to understand in this sentence is that the action verb is passive voice. We have the option of saying either that the beam hit the ship (active voice) or that the ship was hit by the beam (passive voice). Remember that active voice will be preferred in most of the things that you write. A linking verb is neither active voice nor passive voice; these terms apply only to action verbs.

## BINARY DIAGRAM

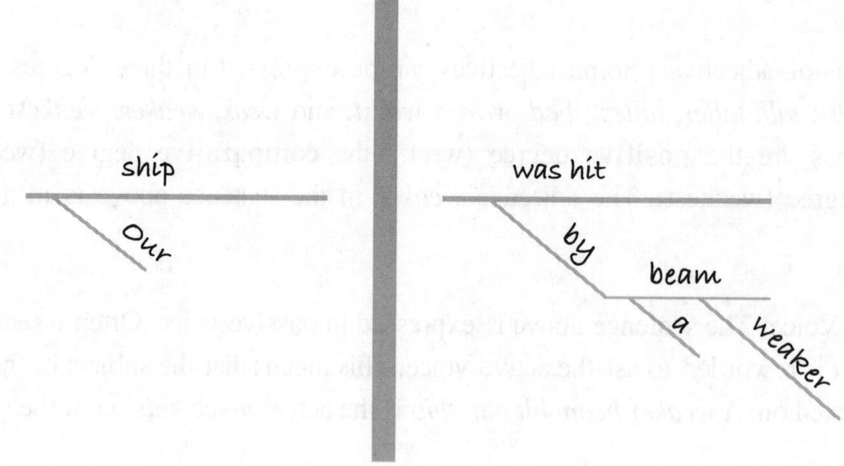

## Questions for individual thought or small group discussion:

**emotion: feelings**

How many names of emotions can you think of? Can you give names to some of the subtle, in-between emotions, e.g. *wistful*? Think of more examples, decide what part of speech each example is, and imagine what someone's face would look like if he or she were experiencing that emotion.

**synthesis: making connections**

What writing function do adjectives, prepositional phrases, adverbs, participle phrases, and infinitive phrases share?

**divergence: thinking of alternatives**

How many descriptive adjectives can you think of that are not the names of colors but that describe visual properties, e.g.,. *shiny*. Keep thinking of examples until you think of some excellent words that are rarely used.

**analysis: breaking down into components**

A traditional sentence diagram has a long horizontal line, dividing the bottom from the top, and a vertical line, dividing the left from the right. What is the difference between these two lines, and which do you think is more important?

Use the grammar clues to solve this Mystery Sentence:

This sentence from a nursery rhyme begins with four alliterated one-syllable interjections in a row, followed by a first person singular subject pronoun, an present tense transitive action verb, a definite article, a singular common noun, a preposition that does not show a relationship of time or of space, an indefinite article, and a three-syllable proper noun.

From Frederick Douglass's

# *Narrative of the Life of Frederick Douglass*

From this time I was most narrowly watched. If I was in a separate room any considerable length of time, I was sure to be suspected of having a book, and was at once called to give an account of myself. All this, however, was too late. The first step had been taken. Mistress, in teaching me the alphabet, had given me the *inch*, and no precaution could prevent me from taking the *ell*.

What characterizes the style of this first paragraph from Frederick Douglass's classic autobiography? How many sentences are in the paragraph? How long are the sentences? Are there many direct objects or subject complements? How many adjectives or adverbs are in the paragraph? Do you see any verbals? What generalizations could you make about the style of the paragraph? Are there needless words in the paragraph, or does every word tell?

How does the writing style of Douglass's paragraph compare to Nathaniel Hawthorne's style in the passage we read in Loop One?

1. Write a compound exclamatory sentence which uses a coordinating conjunction and punctuation to separate the clauses, and which contains one clause with a compound predicate. One of the clauses should contain two adverbs.

2. Write a simple interrogative sentence with a future tense verb, an infinitive phrase, and a prepositional phrase.

# Loop Two Writing Lab
# The Paragraph

1. Write a well-organized paragraph on the subject of your choice. The paragraph should contain at least five sentences.

2. Divide the paragraph into its individual sentences and rearrange them so that the paragraph is as disorganized and confusing as possible. Do this without altering the sentences themselves.

3. Think carefully about what the difference is between paragraphs one and two.

4. Write a well-organized paragraph on the subject, "What Connects One Idea to Another?"

## "Take me home to Aunt Em!"

## -L. Frank Baum

One of the most popular stories ever written, L. Frank Baum's classic about Dorothy and the Wizard of Oz has become a permanent fixture in modern culture. This sentence, uttered with Toto in her arms, reflects Dorothy's profound desire to go home.

**Parts of speech**: *Take* is a singular present tense action verb; *me* is a first person singular object pronoun; *home* is an adverb modifying *take*; *to* is a preposition showing the relationship between its object *Aunt Em* and the verb; *Aunt Em* is a proper noun, which is probably best considered as a single entity.

**Parts of the sentence**: The subject of the sentence is an understood *you*; that subject's predicate is *take*; *me* is the direct object of the action verb.

**Phrases**: There is an adverbial prepositional phrase *to Aunt Em*, that modifies the verb.

**Clauses**: This is a simple imperative sentence; it might be argued that it is an exclamatory sentence, which in a sense is true, but its essence as a command seems to be primary.

## FOUR-LEVEL ANALYSIS

| | (you) | Take | me | home | to | Aunt Em! |
|---|---|---|---|---|---|---|
| **Parts of Speech:** | | v. | pron. | adv. | prep. | n. |
| **Parts of Sentence:** | (subj.) | pred. | direct object | | | |
| **Phrases:** | | | | | ----prepositional phrase---- | |
| **Clauses:** | one independent clause, simple imperative sentence | | | | | |

For each of the next ten sentences, identify the **part of speech** of the word in **bold**:

1. **Polychrome** sculptures have more colors than monochrome ones. ______________
2. The **formation** of troops in formal uniforms was impressive. ______________
3. Three consecutive sequels were of no **consequence**. ______________
4. **His** hypoglycemia made him watch his diet. ______________
5. The patient's hemophilia made it difficult to stop **the** hemorrhage. ______________
6. The expedition's Ultima Thule was the **North** Pole. ______________
7. She felt that it was **infra dig** to eat fried chicken with her fingers. ______________
8. Leukemia produces an **excessive** number of leucocytes. ______________
9. If **hemolysis** breaks down red blood cells, what does analysis do? ______________
10. Did mesons strike Mesopotamia in the **Mesozoic** Era? ______________

For each of the next ten sentences, identify the **part of sentence** of the word in **bold**:

11. Would **you** walk a millimeter to drink a milligram of milk? ______________
12. The memo helped **him** remember the commemoration ceremony. ______________
13. Don't digress; discuss **progress** with members of congress. ______________
14. The collaborators spent laborious **nights** in the laboratory. ______________
15. The mycardiograph showed his myocardium is **strong**. ______________
16. The evacuation left **vacancies** in the vacation resort. ______________
17. The oligarchy gave national **policy** a renewed secrecy. ______________
18. Did the fructose from the apples raise his glucose **level**? ______________
19. Unfortunately, the neurosis **developed** into a psychosis. ______________
20. The celebrity's **pulchritude** was only equaled by his turpitude. ______________

For the next ten sentences, identify the phrase in **bold**:

1. A pleochroic crystal shows colors **from different directions**. ____________
2. **Quivering with anger**, the podiatrist treated the injured arthropod. ____________
3. The sorority was located **between two fraternities**. ____________
4. **Careful searching** showed not one phenomenon but several. ____________
5. The valedictory address contained valid arguments **to think about**. ____________
6. **Finally trapped**, the parapsychologist told a parable with a paradox. ____________
7. Von Helmsmit, **the old baron**, was dominant over his dominion. ____________
8. Do workers **in this country** want a meritocracy or an ergatocracy? ____________
9. Rhizophagous animals dig up and feed **on delicious rhizomes**. ____________
10. Saprogenic bacteria caused the material **to decay rapidly**. ____________

For the next ten sentences, identify the sentence structure (disregard the bold type):

11. The **schism** in the party healed, and they won the election. ____________
12. When he's in **Mesopotamia**, he uses the **hippodrome**. ____________
13. Did his **chromosome** problem have a **psychosomatic** cause? ____________
14. The **Sporozoa** are **Protozoa**; they multiply by **sporogenesis**. ____________
15. The people in the **station** voted to preserve the **status quo**. ____________
16. As we climbed, **rhododendron** bloomed on the high mountainsides. ____________
17. The **taxidermist** was interested in a new **taxonomy** of species. ____________
18. The new **volunteer** had a **malevolent** expression, if you ask me. ____________
19. As the candidate tried to **fraternize**, the local politicians laughed. ____________
20. **Trichinosis** is a disease; it is caused by the **trichina** worm. ____________

For each of the following sentences, circle the letter of each answer that is true. The answer can be any combination, including all or none. This exercise will teach you the real process of punctuation as a function of grammar.

1. With a subtle sort of smile the president said All citizens are created equal.

   a. a comma after the prepositional phrases
   b. an apostrophe in the contraction
   c. a comma before the direct quotation
   d. quotation marks around the direct quotation
   e. a period inside the closing quotation marks

2. When the poet wrote The Divine Comedy he created a new poetic form.

   a. a comma after the independent clause
   b. an apostrophe in the possessive noun
   c. a comma after the dependent clause
   d. italics on the poem title
   e. quotation marks around the poem title

3. A two thirds Roman majority wanted circuses bread and gladiatorial entertainment.

   a. a hyphen in the compound adjective
   b. a colon at the beginning of the list
   c. a comma after the plural common noun
   d. a list comma before the coordinating conjunction
   e. a comma after the dependent clause

4. Reaching blindly outward the hoary translucent apparition gained its footing.

   a. a comma after the prepositional phrase
   b. comma between adjectives preceding the noun
   c. a comma after the participle phrase
   d. a comma after the gerund phrase
   e. an apostrophe in the contraction

5. Ola is the Spanish word for wave it is an easy noun to learn.

   a. quotation marks around the Spanish noun
   b. italics on the Spanish noun
   c. a comma after the independent clause
   d. a comma after the dependent clause
   e. a semicolon after the independent clause

## Explosions and cataclysms rocked the night thunderously.

**Parts of speech**: *Explosions* and *cataclysms* are plural common nouns joined by the coordinating conjunction *and*; *rocked* is a past tense transitive action verb; *the* is an adjective (definite article) modifying the noun *night*; and *thunderously* is an adverb which modifies the verb *rocked*.

**Parts of the sentence**: *Explosions and cataclysms* is the compound subject of the verb *rocked*; *night* is the direct object of the verb *rocked*, since it receives the action of the verb: the night gets rocked. There are no indirect objects or subject complements. Remember that there can be no direct object unless there is an action verb, and there can be no subject complement unless there is a linking verb.

**Phrases**: There are no prepositional, verbal, or appositive phrases.

**Clauses**: This is a simple sentence because it contains only one subject/predicate set, the set *Explosions and cataclysms/rocked*. Notice that even though there are two subjects, they are both subjects of the same verb, and so both belong in the same clause. In order for the two subjects to be in two clauses, they would each have to have their own verb.

• • •

Adverb: the adverb *thunderously* is separated from the verb it modifies by two intervening words. Adverbs have a way of turning up at various locations in sentences.

Punctuation: There should be no comma between the two nouns in the compound subject. Compound sentences sometimes use commas, but compound subjects or verbs do not. Another way of saying this is that if a part of a sentence is compound, it is usually not interrupted with a comma.

## FOUR-LEVEL ANALYSIS

**Explosions and cataclysms rocked the night thunderously.**

| | Explosions | and | cataclysms | rocked | the | night | thunderously. |
|---|---|---|---|---|---|---|---|
| **Parts of Speech:** | n. | conj. | n. | v. | adj. | n. | adv. |
| **Parts of Sentence:** | --------------subject-------------- | | | predicate | | direct object | |
| **Phrases:** | no prepositional, appositive, or verbal phrases | | | | | | |
| **Clauses:** | one independent clause, simple declarative sentence | | | | | | |

## BINARY DIAGRAM

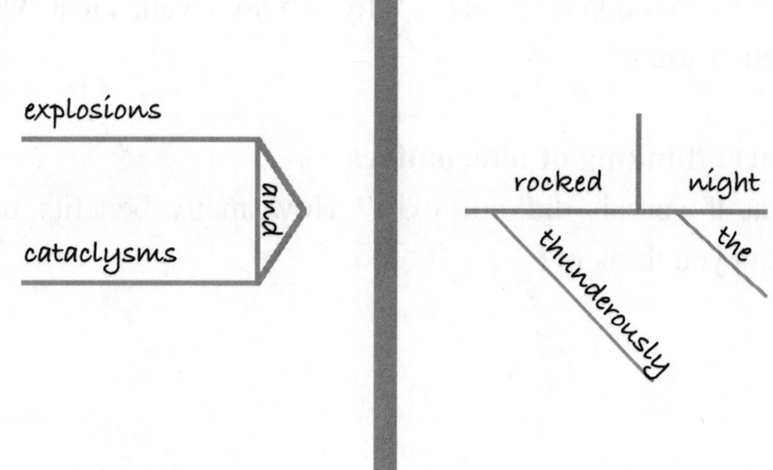

## Questions for individual thought or small group discussion:

**evaluation: judging value with criteria**

Which would be worse, writing characterized by good grammar and poor diction, or writing characterized by good diction and poor grammar? Explain.

**intuition: ideas from the blue**

Language is, among other things, sound. Poets and novelists alike have long recognized that the sounds of words can amplify the emotional power of language. Pick several vowels and several consonants—what images or experiences do the sounds of these letters remind you of? Allow your mind to be free and suggestible, responsive to the sheer elemental sounds of language.

**aesthetics: artistic qualities**

What do you think some people mean by "clean, clear writing"? What would the opposite be? Why would clean, clear writing be considered pleasing?

**divergence: thinking of alternatives**

What if verbals did not exist? How many benefits of having verbals can you think of?

Use the grammar clues to solve this Mystery Sentence:

This sentence from American history begins with a plural demonstrative pronoun, followed by a plural present tense linking verb, then a definite article, then a one-syllable plural common noun; this is followed by a relative clause beginning with a relative pronoun which is also sometimes a singular demonstrative pronoun, a plural present tense action verb, a possessive adjective based on the plural of the noun *man*, and a direct object made of a one-syllable plural common noun rhyming with *rolls*.

From Robert Louis Stevenson's

# *Treasure Island*

I remember him as if it were yesterday, as he came plodding to the inn door, his sea-chest following behind him in a handbarrow; a tall, strong, heavy, not-brown man; his tarry pigtail falling over the shoulders of his soiled blue coat; his hands ragged and scarred, with black, broken nails; and the sabre cut across one cheek, a dirty, livid white.

What can be said about the style of this paragraph from Robert Louis Stevenson's classic sea novel? How many sentences are in the paragraph? What is the sentence structure? Does Stevenson avoid adjectives? What generalizations could you make about the style of the paragraph?

How does Stevenson's writing style compare to Frederick Douglass's or Nathaniel Hawthorne's styles in the selections we saw in Loop One and Loop Two?

Why do you think Stevenson chose this unusual sentence structure?

1. Write a sentence that contains a properly used semicolon and a participle phrase.

2. Write a simple declarative sentence that begins with a first person singular subject pronoun, followed by a singular transitive action verb, then a common noun, followed by a preposition, an adjective definite article, a singular common noun, a preposition modifying that noun, a definite article, and the four-word proper name of a nation, the last two words of which are a prepositional phrase.

# Loop Three Writing Lab
## Sentence Structure

1. Write a paragraph of 50-100 words, in which every sentence is a simple, declarative sentence.

2. Rewrite the paragraph, using various techniques, to make it one sentence.

3. Compare the two versions of the same paragraph.

4. Write a statement about the effect of sentence structure on the feeling of a paragraph.

# It's a sin to kill a mockingbird.

## -Harper Lee

A novel by Harper Lee, *To Kill a Mockingbird*, is known by a statement that is made by one of the novel's characters, Atticus Finch: "It's a sin to kill a mockingbird." Analyze the grammar of Atticus's words.

---

**Parts of speech**: *It's* is a contraction of the third person singular personal pronoun *It* and the present tense linking verb *is*; *a* is an adjective (indefinite article) modifying the singular common noun *sin*; *to kill* is an infinitive adjective modifying *sin*; *a* is an adjective modifying the singular common noun *mockingbird*.

**Parts of the sentence**: The subject of this sentence is *It*, and the predicate is *is*; since *is* is a linking verb, we must look to see if there is a subject complement: yes, *sin* is a subject complement linked to the subject *It* by the linking verb *is*.

**Phrases**: The sentence contains a famous phrase: "to kill a mockingbird." It is an infinitive phrase, and the entire phrase, not just *to kill*, is an adjective modifying *sin*. Within the phrase, *mockingbird* serves as an object to the infinitive *to kill*, as though *to kill* were a verb. Actually, infinitives are never used as verbs in sentences (I to see you!).

**Clauses**: Since the sentence contains only one subject/predicate set, *It/is*, it is a simple sentence by structure. By purpose, the sentence is declarative.

## FOUR-LEVEL ANALYSIS

| | **It's** | **a** | **sin** | **to kill** | **a** | **mockingbird.** |
|---|---|---|---|---|---|---|
| **Parts of Speech:** | pron./v. | adj. | n. | adj. | adj. | n. |
| **Parts of Sentence:** | subj./pred. | | subject complement | | | |
| **Phrases:** | | | | ------------- | infinitive phrase | -------------- |
| **Clauses:** | | one independent clause, simple declarative sentence | | | | |

Identify the **part of speech** in **bold** in these sentences:

1. In the tropics the leafy **heliotropes** turn toward the sun. __________
2. A gastrologist studies the stomach; a **gastronome** prepares food. __________
3. The aged arthropod suffered **from** arthritis and arthralgia. __________
4. The popular ventriloquist had a heart operation on his **left** ventricle. __________
5. **Dorsiventral** leaves have distinct upper and lower surfaces. __________
6. The universe is sometimes referred to as the **macrocosm**. __________
7. Are right-handed people really more **dexterous**? __________
8. **Brachypterous** insects have short wings. __________
9. **Brachiate** trees have widely spreading branches in pairs, like arms. __________
10. The branchiopods are marine crustaceans that breathe **through** gills. __________

Identify the **part of sentence** in **bold** in these sentences:

11. The hyperkinetic boy did not possess **telekinesis**, fortunately. __________
12. The species *Homo sapiens* **belongs** to the Chordata phylum. __________
13. **Reproduction** by budding is also called blastogenesis. __________
14. If fingerprinting is dactylography, is sign language **dactylology**? __________
15. If you press your closed **eyelids**, you will see phosphenes. __________
16. What **is** the difference between a pentagram and a pentagon? __________
17. Perlite is a volcanic **glass** that resembles obsidian. __________
18. The voracious carnivore devoured the small **herbivore**. __________
19. The hologram gave the **scientists** a new view of the structure. __________
20. The diploid **structure** divided into two haploid structures. __________

Identify the type of **phrase** that is in **bold**:

1. Ishmael, **a member of the Anglican church**, is an Anglophile. ______________
2. **To gain insight**, the anthropologist studies human cultures. ______________
3. **Resembling birds**, the pterosaur and pterodactyl were dinosaurs. ______________
4. Pithecanthropus skeletons were found **to be fragile**. ______________
5. Her calligraphy is ornate, like the music **of the calliope**. ______________
6. The austral winds raised storms **over the Australian outback**. ______________
7. **Trembling nervously**, a boy held the cephalopod in both hands. ______________
8. The physician asked the chiropractor **to practice chiromancy**. ______________
9. The survivor **of the holocaust** made a caustic comment. ______________
10. **With a laugh**, the extraterrestrial admired the subterranean grottoes. ______________

Identify the **sentence structure** of each of these sentences. Disregard the bold.

11. The **cataract** and **cataclysm** caused **catastrophe** in the **catacombs**. ______________
12. The lying criminal **perjured** himself, but the **jury** listened. ______________
13. A **confluence** of **influences** made her **fluent** in Spanish, and it did. ______________
14. The senator's **adherents** laughed, and the speech was **incoherent**. ______________
15. The corrupt ruler was **deposed** when his **deposits** were discovered. ______________
16. His **mundane** conversation bored her to tears; it was too much. ______________
17. Is a **democracy** a **meritocracy** or a **plutocracy** for the **aristocracy**? ______________
18. His **egomania** kept him from noticing the **kleptomania** of his guest. ______________
19. Because he was **victimized** by his own ignorance, he paid a price. ______________
20. The **anthology** article discussed the **anthozoans**; it was good. ______________

For each of the following sentences, circle the letter of each answer that is true. The answer can be any combination, including all or none. This exercise will teach you the real process of punctuation as a function of grammar.

1. The Red River Valley is a nice tune to know when youre in the desert.
   a. italics on the song title
   b. quotation marks around the song title
   c. a comma after the dependent clause
   d. a comma after the independent clause
   e. an apostrophe in the contraction

2. Wow its fun to see three countries in a five day trip.
   a. a comma after the interjection
   b. an apostrophe in the possessive pronoun
   c. an apostrophe in the contraction
   d. a comma after the independent clauses
   e. a hyphen in the compound adjective

3. In the Jamestown colony the incidence of pneumonia was down by one third.
   a. comma after the introductory prepositional phrase
   b. a hyphen in the fraction
   c. a comma after the dependent clause
   d. commas around the appositive
   e. commas around the parenthetical remark

4. On December 4 1866 Wassily Kandinsky the abstract painter was born.
   a. a comma after the day
   b. a comma after the year appositive
   c. a comma after the participle phrase
   d. commas around the appositive
   e. a comma after the dependent clause

5. Caught by the swift current Dagoo gazed through the porthole.
   a. a comma after the dependent clause
   b. comma after the introductory prepositional phrases
   c. a comma after the participle phrase
   d. commas around the appositive
   e. a semicolon between the clauses

## The Andromedans attacked savagely, and we fell back.

**Parts of speech**: *The* is an adjective modifying the proper noun *Andromedans*; *attacked* is an intransitive action verb modified by the adverb *savagely*; *and* is a coordinating conjunction which joins two clauses; *we* is a pronoun (a personal, first-person plural pronoun, antecedent unknown); *fell* is the verb of the subject *we*; and *back* is an adverb modifying *fell*.

**Parts of the sentence**: This is an easy sentence to analyze because it simply contains two subject/predicate sets with a few modifiers. The first subject/predicate set is *Andromedans /attacked*, and the second set is *we/fell*. There are no direct objects, indirect objects, or subject complements.

**Phrases**: The sentence contains no prepositional, verbal, or appositive phrases.

**Clauses**: This is a compound sentence because it contains two independent clauses. The first clause is *The Andromedans attacked savagely*, and the second clause is *we fell back*. The two independent clauses are joined by a comma and a coordinating conjunction. Remember that when a compound sentence is joined by a coordinating conjunction (*and, but, or, nor, for, so, yet*), the comma is required. Without the comma the sentence would be a run-on sentence—a major error.

• • •

Compounds: Remember that the most important issue in compounds—whether it is compound adjectives, compound subjects, compound direct objects, or a compound sentence like this one where two independent clauses are joined together into a compound—is not have we punctuated the compound correctly but should this be a compound in the first place. We make compounds so that sentences will reflect the real world, where things sometimes come in pairs. This includes ideas, events, and objects.

## FOUR-LEVEL ANALYSIS

| | The | Andromedans | attacked | savagely, | and | we | fell | back. |
|---|---|---|---|---|---|---|---|---|
| **Parts of Speech:** | adj. | n. | v. | adv. | conj. | pron. | v. | adv. |
| **Parts of Sentence:** | | subject | predicate | | | | | |
| **Phrases:** | no prepositional, appositive, or verbal phrases | | | | | | | |
| **Clauses:** | -------------independent clause------------- | | | | | --independent clause-- | | |
| | two independent clauses, I,ccI compound declarative sentence | | | | | | | |

This sentence illustrates the proper construction of an I,ccI compound sentence, with the comma before the coordinating conjunction that joins the two clauses together.

## BINARY DIAGRAM

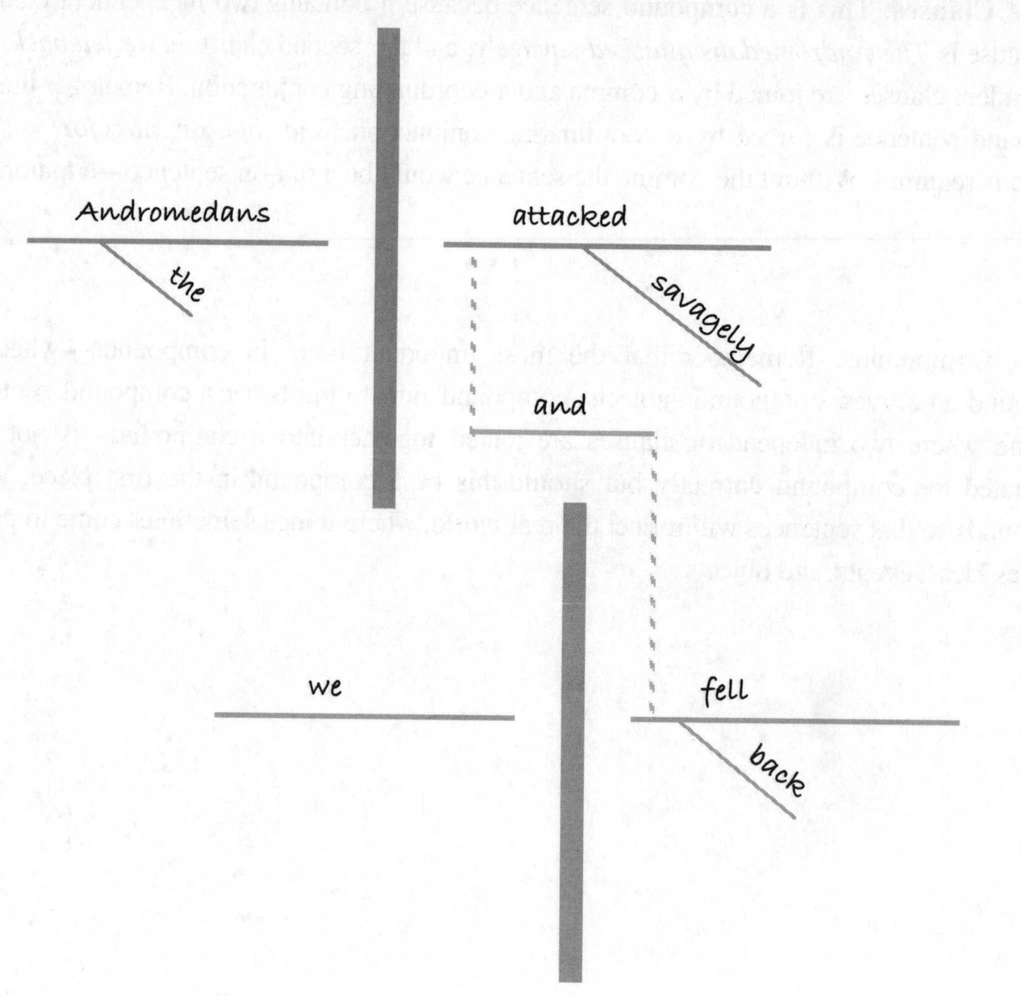

## Questions for individual thought or small group discussion:

**analysis: breaking down into components**

The word *paragraph* is composed of two ancient stems, *para*, meaning beside, and *graph*, meaning write. Explain, in terms of these stems, why the name paragraph is an excellent name for what a paragraph does.

**evaluation: judging value with criteria**

One of our alternatives in writing is to choose between the indirect object and the prepositional phrase. We can say *I present Mort this medal* or *I present this medal to Mort.* If you were addressing an awards banquet, which construction would you prefer to use, and why?

**intuition: ideas from the blue**

Pick a color adjective, a motion adjective, and a temperature adjective. Imagine a scene which those three adjectives suggest.

**synthesis: making connections**

What two parts of speech do you think have most in common? What two parts of sentence do you think have most in common? Give your reasons. What grammar structure reminds you most of something in mathematics?

Use the grammar clues to solve this Mystery Sentence:

This interrogative sentence from a children's nursery rhyme begins with a two-syllable proper noun, repeated twice and used as the noun of direct address, followed by an adverb modifying an adjective that rhymes with the first word of the sentence, then an interrogative adverb, a helping verb, a second person singular possessive pronoun, a two-syllable common noun, and a main verb.

From Henry David Thoreau's

# *Walden*

The adventurous student will always study classics, in whatever language they may be written and however ancient they may be. For what are the classics but the noblest recorded thoughts of man? They are the only oracles which are not decayed, and there are such answers to the most modern inquiry in them as Delphi and Dodona never gave. We might as well omit to study Nature because she is old. To read well, that is, to read true books in a true spirit, is a noble exercise, and one that will task the reader more than any exercise which the customs of the day esteem. It requires a training such as the athletes underwent, the steady intention almost of the whole life to this object. Books must be read as deliberately and reservedly as they were written.

What do you notice about the style of this paragraph from Henry David Thoreau's classic essay? How long are Thoreau's sentences? Does he use big words, or rely on common words? What is the central purpose of this paragraph? Which sentence do you think is the best expression of his theme? How many verbals does Thoreau use?

1. Write a compound imperative sentence that has no pronouns, but has a noun of direct address and two interjections.

2. Write a simple declarative sentence that has a compound infinitive as the subject of a linking verb, with a subject complement (predicate nominative form) following the verb.

# Loop Four Writing Lab
## Verbals

1. Write twenty-five words, using only sentences and no sentence fragments, containing as many verbals as you can possibly fit in.

2. Rewrite the passage, trying to replace every verbal with a common noun.

3. Compare the two versions of the same paragraph.

4. Write a statement explaining what you learned about verbals.

## "I'm sure those are not the right words."

## -Lewis Carroll

In Wonderland, Alice says this after trying unsuccessfully to recite a poem about a crocodile. The grammar is very interesting.

**Parts of speech**: *I'm* is the contraction of the subject pronoun *I* and the singular present tense linking verb *am*; *sure* is an adjective modifying *I*; *those* is a plural demonstrative pronoun; *are* is a plural present tense linking verb *are*: *not* is an adverb modifying *are*; *the* is an adjective definite article modifying the plural common noun *words*; and *right* is also an adjective modifying *words*.

**Parts of the sentence**: *I* is the subject of the linking verb predicate *am*, which links the subject to a subject complement predicate adjective *sure*; in the second clause, *those* is the subject of the linking verb *are* which links its subject to the subject complement predicate nominative *words*.

**Phrases**: There are no prepositional, appositive, or verbal phrases.

**Clauses**: This short sentence has a main clause, *I'm sure*, followed by an adverbial clause *those are not the right words* that modifies the adjective *sure*.

### FOUR-LEVEL ANALYSIS

| | I'm | sure | those | are | not | the | right | words. |
|---|---|---|---|---|---|---|---|---|
| **Parts of Speech:** | pron./v. | adj. | pron. | v. | adv. | adj. | adj. | n. |
| **Parts of Sentence:** | subj./pred. | subject complement | subj. | pred. | | | | subject complement |
| **Phrases:** | ----no prepositional, appositive, or verbal phrases---- | | | | | | | |
| **Clauses:** | an ID complex declarative sentence | | | | | | | |

Identify the **part of speech** in **bold** in each sentence below:

1. The linguini-loving linguist knew the **lingua franca**. ____________
2. **Motile** microorganisms have powers of spontaneous motion. ____________
3. The navy **circumnavigated** the globe by precise navigation. ____________
4. The **undulant** waves soon inundated the low regions. ____________
5. The famous **polyglot** spoke seventeen languages. ____________
6. A hazy corona circled the moon the night **before** the coronation. ____________
7. The goddess of the golden dawn, Aurora, held the **auriferous** rocks. ____________
8. At the party the **literati** discussed the glories of literature. ____________
9. The rational person will not **rationalize** his wrongs away. ____________
10. Singing was an emotional **catharsis** for the vocalist. ____________

Identify the **part of sentence** in **bold** in each sentence below:

11. There **was** a disparity between his story and the facts. ____________
12. Are the rewards of the job **commensurate** with the duties? ____________
13. We can choose either harmony or **acrimony**. ____________
14. The quintet played **Mozart** to a group of quinquagenarians. ____________
15. The **sociopath** used his knowledge of sociology to evil purposes. ____________
16. Ovoviviparous fish produce **eggs** that hatch inside the mother. ____________
17. The **dysphasia** resulted from injury to the brain's speech center. ____________
18. His resignation **obviated** the need for impeachment proceedings. ____________
19. Are you studying these phenomena or this **phenomenon**? ____________
20. Histology is the **study** of the structure of plant and animal tissues. ____________

For each sentence, identify the type of **phrase** in **bold**:

1. The atmometer measures the rate **of evaporation** of water. ________
2. **Completely fascinated**, the cardiologist saw the electrocardiogram. ________
3. **For a technician**, the Soviet cosmonaut had cosmopolitan tastes. ________
4. The order **to attack quickly** was countermanded by his counterpart. ________
5. The craniotomy was performed **by a skilled brain surgeon**. ________
6. As if **to make a point**, the cyclone hurled the bicycle fifty yards. ________
7. Agnostics are not usually attracted **to Gnosticism**. ________
8. Over the years, his habits had ossified **beyond hope of change**. ________
9. Beetles, **xylophagous insects**, had eaten the antique xylophone. ________
10. The costermonger and fishmonger shouted out prices **to passersby**. ________

For each sentence, identify the **sentence structure**. Disregard bold type.

11. **September** was the seventh month of the Roman calendar. ________
12. I know; the flood of immigration stirred the public **xenophobia**. ________
13. The **cardiovascular** system responded as the exercise increased. ________
14. The storm **forecast** filled her with **foreboding**, but it was not enough. ________
15. When she looked, the **smallish** object had a faint, **greenish** tint. ________
16. Their assault on the summit was **hopeless**, **bootless**, and **fruitless**. ________
17. As you know, we think high fashion is a **barometer** for new trends. ________
18. The geologist studied the **ferrous** rock with care, but he missed it. ________
19. The **quasi-military** operation into Cambodia has failed; it is true. ________
20. We visited **Polynesia**, **Micronesia**, and **Melanesia** and came home. ________

For each of the following sentences, circle the letter of each answer that is true. The answer can be any combination, including all or none. This exercise will teach you the real process of punctuation as a function of grammar.

1. In December Baltimore lost its best player when a bizarre event occurred.

   a. a comma after the prepositional phrase
   b. a comma after the month
   c. an apostrophe in the possessive pronoun
   d. an apostrophe in the contraction
   e. a comma between the clauses

2. Because the wind was roaring we remained on the beach.

   a. a comma after the participle phrase
   b. a comma after the dependent clause
   c. a comma after the independent clause
   d. a semicolon between the clauses
   e. a comma after the prepositional phrase

3. The well intentioned athlete ran two miles uphill one downhill and one level.

   a. a hyphen in the compound adjective
   b. a colon before the list
   c. a comma after the adjective uphill
   d. a list comma after the adjective downhill
   e. a comma between the clauses

4. Flying across the Pacific was Noonans greatest dream.

   a. a comma after the introductory participle phrase
   b. a comma after the dependent clause
   c. an apostrophe in the possessive noun
   d. commas around the appositive phrase
   e. commas around the parenthetical remark

5. Yes the English lost twenty five fighters in the Battle of Britain.

   a. a comma after the introductory adverb
   b. a comma after the interjection
   c. a comma after the dependent clause
   d. a hyphen in the compound adjective
   e. a comma before the prepositional phrase

## Every planet has a magnetic field around it.

**Parts of speech**: *Every* is an adjective modifying the singular common noun *planet*; *has* is a present tense active voice transitive action verb; *a* is an adjective (indefinite article) modifying the singular common noun *field*; *magnetic* is also an adjective modifying the noun *field*; *around* is a preposition; and *it* is a third person singular pronoun which takes the place of the noun *planet*. In other words, *planet* is the antecedent of *it*.

**Parts of the sentence**: The subject is *planet*; the simple predicate is *has*; and the direct object is *field*.

**Phrases**: The sentence contains only one prepositional phrase, *around it*. The phrase modifies the verb *has*, telling where.

**Clauses**: The sentence contains only one clause, and it is therefore a simple sentence.

• • •

Subject/Verb Agreement: The adjective *every* before a subject takes a singular verb. This is true regardless of intervening prepositional phrases: *Every* one of the planets *has* a magnetic field around it. Every one/has, not Every one/have.

To have: The verb *has* is sometimes mistaken for a linking verb, since it sounds so much like *is*. But notice that the sentence doesn't link the planet to the field: it isn't an equation; the field isn't something the planet IS; the field is something the planet has. The planet has a field, just as a man has a duck. The field and the duck are objects which receive the action of the verb, they are not subject complements which are linked to (identified with) the subject. Possession, in other words, is a form of action.

## FOUR-LEVEL ANALYSIS

| | Every | planet | has | a | magnetic | field | around | it. |
|---|---|---|---|---|---|---|---|---|
| **Parts of Speech:** | adj. | n. | v. | adj. | adj. | n. | prep. | pron. |
| **Parts of Sentence:** | | subject | predicate | | | direct object | | |
| **Phrases:** | | | | | | | --prepositional-- | |
| **Clauses:** | one independent clause, simple declarative sentence | | | | | | | |

Prepositional phrases are always modifiers: adjectives or adverbs. How do we know that this phrase is an adverb and not an adjective? We can hear the logic: it has it around it, sounds more right than a field around it. And the phrase tells where the planet *has* it.

## BINARY DIAGRAM

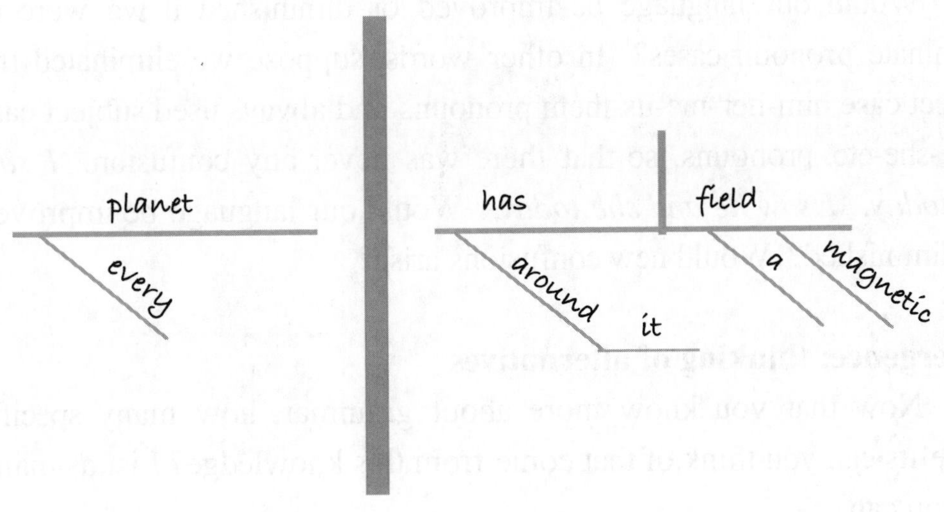

## Questions for individual thought or small group discussion:

**analysis: breaking down into components**

The word **participle** comes from the Latin word *participium*, meaning a participation—a sharing. In what sense is there a participation in the relationship between a noun or pronoun and its participle?

**aesthetics: artistic qualities**

You are in telepathic communication with a friendly alien on a distant desert planet. The mind-pal can understand the words of your thoughts but cannot see visions through your eyes. What nouns, adjectives, and adverbs can you use to help your friend understand what rain is like, as we experience it through our senses? Answer this question by listing first the nouns, then the adjectives, and then the adverbs which communicate the experience of rain.

**evaluation: judging value with criteria**

Would our language be improved or diminished if we were to eliminate pronoun cases? In other words, suppose we eliminated the object case him-her-me-us-them pronouns and always used subject case I-he-she-etc. pronouns, so that there was never any confusion. *I saw he today. I saw he and she today.* Would our language be improved or diminished? Would new confusions arise?

**divergence: thinking of alternatives**

Now that you know more about grammar, how many specific benefits can you think of that come from this knowledge? List as many as you can.

Use the grammar clues to solve this Mystery Sentence:

A famous sentence from Shakespeare begins with a compound infinitive in which the second infinitive in the compound is negated by an adverb and ends with a clause that contains a demonstrative pronoun as a subject, a present tense linking verb, a definite article, and a singular common noun as a subject complement.

From George Orwell's

# *1984*

Don't you see that the whole aim of Newspeak is to narrow the range of thought? In the end we shall make thoughtcrime literally impossible, because there will be no words in which to express it. Every concept that can ever be needed will be expressed by exactly *one* word, with its meaning rigidly defined and all its subsidiary meanings rubbed out and forgotten.

What can you say about the style of this paragraph from George Orwell's classic novel of a nightmarish totalitarian society? How would you characterize the tone of Orwell's paragraph? Was Orwell implying that control of grammar would be control of society? What is the relationship between individuality and language? How many clauses are there in this paragraph? What is the most common sentence structure?

1. Write a five clause compound sentence that has nine words or fewer.

2. Write a clause of ten words or more that has one noun, one verb, but no conjunctions, no interjections, and no prepositions.

# Loop Five Writing Lab
# Disruptions of Normal Order

1. Write five separate sentences that begin with subjects and then have transitive action verbs and direct objects.

2. Revise each sentence so that the direct object precedes the subject and verb.

3. Compare the two versions of the sentences.

4. Write a statement explaining what you learned about the effect of inverting normal sentence order.

## "In our last conflict, four of his five wits went halting off."

## -William Shakespeare

This scathing line, spoken by Beatrice in Act I scene i of Shakespeare's comedy *Much Ado About Nothing*, shows Beatrice's contempt for the mean intelligence of her rival, Benedick, with whom she is destined to fall in love, like it or not. Its creative wording gives new life to the tired phrase, *lost his wits*.

**Parts of speech**: *In* is a preposition; *our* is a possessive pronoun that also has some force as an adjective; *last* is an adjective modifying the singular common noun *conflict*; *four* is a noun; *of* is a preposition showing the relationship between *wits* and *four*; *his* is a possessive pronoun; *went* is a plural past tense verb; *halting* is an adverb which modifies the verb and is modified by another adverb *off*. If you try to say that *went halting* is the verb, how would you answer the question, what tense is it?

**Parts of the sentence**: The subject of this sentence is *four*; the subject's simple predicate is the action verb *went*. If you try to say that *wits* is the subject, than what is the object of the preposition—an adjective?

**Phrases**: There are two prepositional phrases, *in our last conflict* which modifies the verb, and *of his five wits* which modifies *four*.

**Clauses**: This is a simple declarative sentence, consisting of only one clause, since it has only one subject/predicate set.

## FOUR-LEVEL ANALYSIS

| | In | our | last | conflict, | four | of | his | five | wits | went | halting | off. |
|---|---|---|---|---|---|---|---|---|---|---|---|---|
| **Parts of Speech:** | prep. | pron. | adj. | n. | n. | prep. | pron. | adj. | n. | v. | adv. | adv. |
| **Parts of Sentence:** | | | | | subject | | | | | predicate | | |
| **Phrases:** | -----prepositional phrase----- | | | | | --prep. phrase-- | | | | | | |
| **Clauses:** | one independent clause, simple declarative sentence | | | | | | | | | | | |

For each sentence, identify the **part of speech** of the word in **bold**.

1. We **convened** at the Hilton on Third Avenue. ______________
2. The **ichthyologist** removed the petrified ichthyosaur bones. ______________
3. The **gravamen** of the charges is that he left his post under fire. ______________
4. The calorimeter measured the heat of the **calorific** reaction. ______________
5. **Heliophiles** catch few solar rays at the winter solstice. ______________
6. The ophthalmologist treats the diseases of **the** eye. ______________
7. There were nucleotides in the chromosomes **of** the cell nucleus. ______________
8. He tried **to sate** his insatiable appetite for pizza. ______________
9. Male proterandrous insects appear earlier in the season **than** females. ______________
10. The montane vistas of Montevideo **are** like those in Montana. ______________

For each sentence, identify the **part of sentence** of the word in **bold**.

11. A kilometer, one thousand meters, is 0.62137 **miles** in length. ______________
12. Myriad **explanations** exist of unidentified flying objects. ______________
13. At the first sign of tachycardia, he **was rushed** to the hospital. ______________
14. Is nuclear fission the **opposite** of nuclear fusion? ______________
15. The cumulus clouds accumulated as the sun baked the **sea**. ______________
16. The meteorologist reported that the meteorite did no **damage**. ______________
17. The hibernal winds did not reach the hibernating **bear**. ______________
18. The dilemma **was** whether to study the dicotyledon or diencephalon. ______________
19. The **bathymetry** of the Pacific was easily studied with a bathyscaph. ______________
20. Barnacles and other cirripeds covered the marina's **pilings**. ______________

For each sentence, identify the type of **phrase** in **bold**, and give its part of speech.

1. The gloomy soul was unable **to overcome her melancholy**. ________
2. **Suddenly stumbling**, the vice president greeted the vice consul. ________
3. Agent Orange was a toxic defoliant used **in the Vietnam War**. ________
4. **To provide relief**, we filled the atomizer with a new scent. ________
5. **In morphological terms**, orbicular leaves are circular and flat. ________
6. Her multifarious nefarious deeds landed her **in prison**. ________
7. The ignis fatuus seemed to ignite and hover **over the swamp**. ________
8. We could do nothing **to mollify the man's anger**. ________
9. Quickly delineate your proposal **for the new rapid transit system**. ________
10. Hemiplegia, **a partial paralysis**, is a serious condition. ________

For each sentence, identify the **sentence structure**. Disregard the bold.

11. The obsessed **oologist** painted his house; it was robin's-egg blue. ________
12. As we became aware of the ship's **retrograde** motion, we sank. ________
13. The **pneumococcus** bacteria gave him **pneumonia**, and it was bad. ________
14. Skeletons of the microscopic **radiolarians** show **radial** symmetry. ________
15. The sponge expels water through its **osculum**; this is well known. ________
16. As you saw, the **immense** wall was **impervious** to cannon fire. ________
17. The **convection** current distributed the heat of the flames. ________
18. Houdini accomplished feats of **prestidigitation**, but he was doomed. ________
19. The **gymnasium** is the perfect place for **gymnastics**, or so I think. ________
20. An Amoeba's **cytoplasm** includes **endoplasm** and **ectoplasm**. ________

For each of the following sentences, circle the letter of each answer that is true. The answer can be any combination, including all or none. This exercise will teach you the real process of punctuation as a function of grammar.

1. The Neotitanic the fastest cruise ship on the planet can reach fifty two knots.

a. quotation marks around the ship title
b. italics on the ship title
c. commas around the dependent clause
d. commas around the appositive
e. a hyphen in the compound number

2. Taken by surprise the yellow spider jumped at the arachnologist.

a. a comma after the dependent clause
b. a comma after the gerund phrase
c. a comma after the participle phrase
d. commas around the appositive
e. quotation marks around the subject

3. The new usher who happens to have the letter *m* on his cap is short.

a. a comma after the compound subject
b. commas around the appositive
c. commas around the nonessential clause
d. a semicolon between the independent clauses
e. italics on the letter as such

4. The Virginia colony needed three things salt pepper and catsup.

a. a semicolon between the clauses
b. a colon after the plural noun
c. a comma after **salt**
d. a list comma before the coordinating conjunction
e. commas around the parenthetical remark

5. Did you read the story Digital Literature in this months Electrica Magazine?

a. quotation marks around the story title
b. italics on the story title
c. commas around the appositive
d. italics on the magazine title
e. an apostrophe in the possessive noun

# Grammar Review Test

# Loop 1-5

# Prepare for Usage Questions

The Grammar Review Test is based on the five four-level analyses that are the first pages of each of the five loops. Questions on the test come from all four levels of grammar: parts of speech, parts of the sentence, phrases, and clauses.

In addition to containing seventy-five questions based on four of the five sentences studied in class, the Grammar Review Test will also contain twenty-five other questions on usage, subject-verb agreement, clause punctuation, and other matters covered in the introductory lectures. A thorough review of all previous loops is recommended.

Students should be reminded that on a given question, more than one answer may be true; they should pick the *best*, most complete, answer.

to
be
or
to
be
not
is
Q
the

## This is the desert where the elves decimated the trolls.

**Parts of speech**: *This* is a demonstrative pronoun; *is* is a verb; *the* is an adjective modifying the singular common noun *desert*; *where* is a subordinating conjunction; *the* is an adjective (definite article) modifying the plural common noun *elves*; *decimated* is a verb (past tense, transitive); *the* is an adjective modifying the plural common noun *trolls*.

**Parts of the sentence**: The sentence contains a subject/linking verb/subject complement structure in *This/is/desert*. It also contains a subject/action verb/direct object structure in *elves/decimated/trolls*.

**Phrases**: There are no prepositional, verbal, or appositive phrases.

**Clauses**: This is an ID complex sentence because it contains one independent clause, *This is the desert*, and one dependent clause, *where the elves decimated the trolls*. The clauses are connected by the relative adverb *where*, and the dependent clause is a relative dependent clause whose function is to modify the noun *desert*. In other words, the entire dependent clause functions as an adjective!

• • •

Where: Note that the word *where* is described both as a relative adverb and as a subordinating conjunction. The word serves a dual purpose; it joins the clauses, and it modifies the verb *decimated*.

ID: Remember the punctuation rule for this structure. Since the independent clause comes first, there is no comma.

## FOUR-LEVEL ANALYSIS

| | This | is | the | desert | where | the | elves | decimated | the | trolls. |
|---|---|---|---|---|---|---|---|---|---|---|
| **Parts of Speech:** | pron. | v. | adj. | n. | conj. | adj. | n. | v. | adj. | n. |
| **Parts of Sentence:** | subject | predicate | | subject complement | | | subject | predicate | | direct object |
| **Phrases:** | no prepositional, appositive, or verbal phrases | | | | | | | | | |
| **Clauses:** | ---independent clause--- | | | | -----------------dependent clause-------------------- | | | | | |
| | one independent clause, one dependent clause, ID complex declarative sentence | | | | | | | | | |

## BINARY DIAGRAM

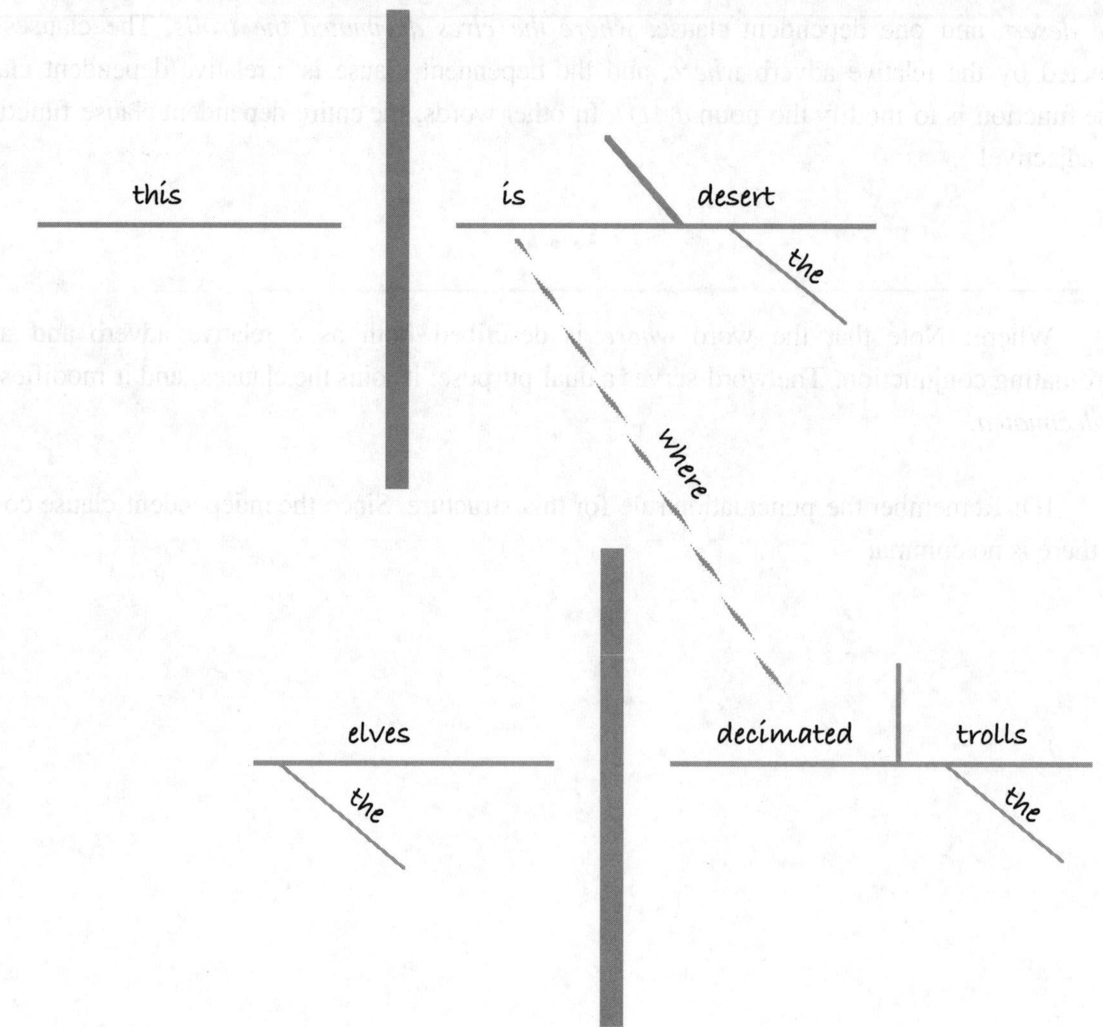

## Questions for individual thought or small group discussion:

**emotion: feelings**

How could you use grammar and diction to make language cold, formal, and impersonal?

**aesthetics: artistic qualities**

What are some of the best adjectives a writer can use to describe olfactory or tactile sense impressions?

**synthesis: making connections**

Imagine a sentence with a common noun, an action verb, and twelve other words, all of them adjectives or adverbs. What, outside of language, does this remind you of?

**analysis: breaking down into components**

Make a long list of prepositions. Then sort the prepositions into different types, such as prepositions of time: before, after, etc. How many different types of prepositions can you find?

Use the grammar clues to solve this Mystery Sentence:

A sentence from a lullaby begins with a four-word dependent clause containing a subordinating conjunction, a definite article, a singular common noun, and an intransitive present tense action verb. This is followed by an independent clause containing a definite article, a singular common noun, and a future tense intransitive action verb.

From Mary Shelley's

# *Frankenstein*

One secret which I alone possessed was the hope to which I had dedicated myself; and the moon gazed on my midnight labours, while, with unrelaxed and breathless eagerness, I pursued nature to her hiding-places. Who shall conceive the horrors of my secret toil, as I dabbled among the unhallowed damps of the grave, or tortured the living animal to animate the lifeless clay? My limbs now tremble, and my eyes swim with the remembrance; but then a resistless, and almost frantic, impulse, urged me forward; I seemed to have lost all soul or sensation but for this one pursuit.

Here is a striking passage from Mary Shelley's immortal monster novel, *Frankenstein*. She wrote the novel at the urging of her husband, the great British poet Percy Shelley, and their friend, the other great British poet George Gordon, Lord Byron. At first writing it as a short story, she later expanded it into a novel. When she began the work, she was nineteen years old. How is this passage different from one you would be likely to write? What do you notice about Shelley's use of sentence structure?

1. Write a sentence that contains six interjections in quotation marks, followed by a proper noun and an intransitive active voice verb.

2. Write a compound sentence with four nouns, all of them verbals; the sentence should contain no conjunction.

# Loop Six Writing Lab: Clause Structure

1. Write two separate sentences that are related in content.

2. Rewrite the sentences, combining them into an I,ccI compound sentence.

3. Rewrite the sentences again, combining them into a D,I complex sentence.

4. Rewrite the sentences again, combining them into an ID complex sentence.

5. Determine which of the variation you think is best, and write a paragraph explaining why.

## "It yearns me not if men my garments wear."

## -William Shakespeare

This sentence, from *Henry V*, IV. iii., expresses the king's priorities. He is not covetous for gold, or material possessions; rather, he is inspired by the idea that "we few, we happy few, we band of brothers" will achieve glory in battle.

**Parts of speech**: *It* is a a third person singular subject pronoun; *yearns* is a present tense active voice transitive action verb; *me* is a first person singular object pronoun; *not* is an adverb modifying the verb; *if* is a subordinating conjunction; *men* is a plural common noun; *my* is a first person singular possessive pronoun; *garments* is a plural common noun; and *wear* is present tense active voice transitive action verb. We do not normally use *years* transitively, as Shakespeare does here.

**Parts of the sentence**: *It* is the subject of the action verb predicate *yearns*, which has *me* as its direct object; *men* is the subject of the action verb predicate *wear*, which has *garments* as its direct object.

**Phrases**: There are no prepositional, appositive, or verbal phrases.

**Clauses**: This is an ID complex declarative sentence; the independent clause is *It yearns me not* and the dependent clause is *if men my garments wear*. The dependent clause is interesting for its word order, which would normally be "if men wear my garments."

### FOUR-LEVEL ANALYSIS

| | **It** | **yearns** | **me** | **not** | **if** | **men** | **my** | **garments** | **wear.** |
|---|---|---|---|---|---|---|---|---|---|
| **Parts of Speech:** | pron. | v. | pron. | adv. | conj. | n. | pron. | n. | v. |
| **Parts of Sentence:** | subj. | pred. | direct object | | | subj. | | direct object | pred. |
| **Phrases:** | ----no prepositional, appositive, or verbal phrases---- | | | | | | | | |
| **Clauses:** | -------independent clause-------- | | | | ----------------dependent clause----------------- | | | | |
| | an ID complex declarative sentence | | | | | | | | |

Identify the **part of speech** in **bold** in each sentence below:

1. The **equivocating** politician praised both groups. ______________
2. A **superfluous** comment is a waste of time. ______________
3. The two nations formed a **bilateral** agreement. ______________
4. A **circumspect** reply is safer. ______________
5. A big job needs a **commensurate** reward. ______________
6. The creature cast a **malevolent** glare. ______________
7. She is a **neophyte** in the art world. ______________
8. The grouchy **misanthropist** wouldn't contribute. ______________
9. The **bellicose** tribe attacked without warning. ______________
10. They believe in an **anthropomorphic** god. ______________

Identify the **part of sentence** in *italics* in each sentence below:

11. The **captious** *remarks* were not sincere. ______________
12. Create a ***neologism***, like televoracious. ______________
13. The convict's muttered **malediction** was *inaudible*. ______________
14. Her **incredulous** expression showed her *feelings*. ______________
15. You can't keep *secrets* from an **omniscient** god. ______________
16. It was a *hobby* that became a **monomania**. ______________
17. You have a convincing but unfortunately **specious** *argument*. ______________
18. His speech **excoriated** the *opponent*. ______________
19. We saw an early ***prototype*** of the Mustang. ______________
20. It is a hostile, **xenophobic** *country*. ______________

For each sentence, identify the type of *phrase* in *italics* and its part of speech:

1. It can be difficult *to **mollify** someone's anger.* ________
2. *Up the bank* splashed a water-logged **ichthyologist**. ________
3. *Speaking seven languages,* she is a brilliant **polyglot**. ________
4. Look *through the **diaphanous** draperies.* ________
5. *The **somniferous** speaking* put him to sleep. ________
6. He has a comfortable **sinecure** *in his uncle's firm.* ________
7. *For modern critics,* Hamlet's famous **soliloquy** is the question. ________
8. The **adherents** *of a militaristic foreign policy* want war. ________
9. ***To abjure** one's former beliefs* is stressful. ________
10. The **caustic** comments *about her clothes* hurt her. ________

For each sentence, identify the **sentence structure**. Disregard bold type.

11. The idea was formed by a **confluence** of other ideas. ________
12. He was **deposed** without violence; everyone approved. ________
13. The offensive **egomaniac** praised himself as we expected. ________
14. When it happened, it was **egregious** act of vandalism. ________
15. Take an extra-strength **analgesic** for the headache, and sleep. ________
16. Try to divine the future through superannuated **chiromancy**. ________
17. The corrupt **oligarchy** kept control when the revolution failed. ________
18. The bigot's **intractable** opinions were unchangeable. ________
19. The **intransigent** true believers wouldn't budge; I know. ________
20. When night fell, his **perfidious** cowardice made him infamous. ________

For each of the following sentences, circle the letter of each answer that is true. The answer can be any combination, including all or none. This exercise will teach you the real process of punctuation as a function of grammar.

1. In the thriving Delaware colony the heavy market in iron tools was raising profits.

a. comma after the introductory prepositional phrase
b. a comma after the dependent clause
c. commas around the parenthetical remark
d. a semicolon between the independent clauses
e. a hyphen in the compound adjective

2. The insects that ate the wooden braces are hard to eliminate.

a. commas around the appositive
b. a semicolon between the independent clauses
c. commas around the nonessential clause
d. quotation marks around the word **braces**
e. a comma before the infinitive

3. Robert Dubious our new senator was opposed however its happening.

a. commas around the appositive
b. a semicolon between the independent clauses
c. a comma after **however**
d. an apostrophe in the contraction
e. a comma after the dependent clause

4. In the winter of 76 the wolfs teeth left marks like letter vs on the windowsill.

a. an apostrophe before the contraction
b. comma after the introductory prepositional phrases
c. an apostrophe in the possessive noun
d. italics on the letter as such
e. an apostrophe in the plural letter as such

5. The heavily loaded jeep careened across the plain.

a. comma between adjectives preceding the subject
b. a comma after the independent clause
c. a semicolon between the independent clauses
d. a comma before the prepositional phrases
e. a comma before the participle phrase

## The meteor struck, and Leonidas smiled stoically.

**Parts of speech**: *The* is an adjective modifying the singular common noun *meteor*; *struck* is an action verb; *and* is a coordinating conjunction; *Leonidas* is a proper noun; *smiled* is a past tense intransitive action verb; and *stoically* is an adverb modifying the verb *smiled.*

**Parts of the sentence**: *meteor* is the subject of the verb *struck*, and *Leonidas* is the subject of the verb *smiled.* There are no subject complements, direct objects, or indirect objects in the sentence.

**Phrases**: There are no prepositional, infinitive, participle, gerund, or appositive phrases in the sentence.

**Clauses**: The sentence is a compound sentence because it contains two independent clauses; the first clause is *The meteor struck*, and the second clause is *Leonidas smiled stoically.* Either clause could be written as a sentence by itself. The two clauses are glued together by the coordinating conjunction *and.*

• • •

Punctuation: The comma before the *and* is necessary in this sentence. It is not always necessary to put a comma before every *and,* but it is necessary to put a comma before every coordinating conjunction *IF* the coordinating conjunction is used to join two independent clauses into a compound sentence. (Note on exceptions: *Extremely* short compound sentences sometimes dispense with the comma, and novelists might omit the comma for creative reasons, as to speed the flow of language, but for normal writing purposes, it is best to always include the comma.)

Leonidas: A famous name in history, Leonidas was the leader of the Spartans at the battle of Thermopylae. We have used his name to pay our respects.

## FOUR-LEVEL ANALYSIS

| | The | meteor | struck, | and | Leonidas | smiled | stoically. |
|---|---|---|---|---|---|---|---|
| **Parts of Speech:** | adj. | n. | v. | conj. | n. | v. | adv. |
| **Parts of Sentence:** | | subject | predicate | | subject | predicate | |
| **Phrases:** | no prepositional, appositive, or verbal phrases | | | | | | |
| **Clauses:** | two independent clauses, compound declarative sentence | | | | | | |

Here is the classic, balanced compound sentence, weighing evenly on both sides of the coordinating conjunction.

## BINARY DIAGRAM

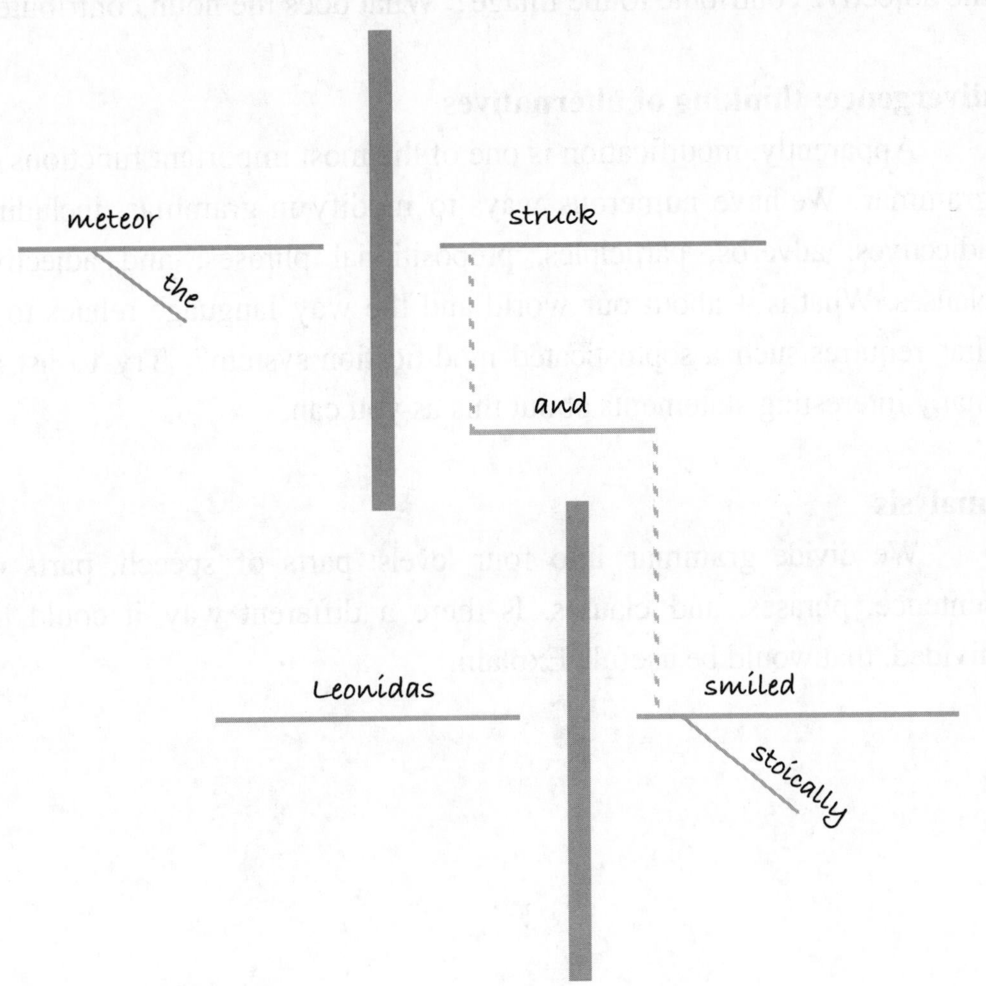

## Questions for individual thought or small group discussion:

**emotion: feelings**

What nouns can you think of which are not the names of emotions but which are clear evidence of emotions, e.g., *grin*?

**intuition: ideas from the blue**

What is suggested to your mind by the following alliterated adjective and noun: *shadowy shape*? Take a minute to let an image develop in your mind, and then explain what it looks like. What does the adjective contribute to the image? What does the noun contribute?

**divergence: thinking of alternatives**

Apparently, modification is one of the most important functions of grammar. We have numerous ways to modify in grammar, including adjectives, adverbs, participles, prepositional phrases, and adjective clauses. What is it about our world and the way language relates to it that requires such a sophisticated modification system? Try to list as many interesting statements about this as you can.

**analysis**

We divide grammar into four levels: parts of speech, parts of sentence, phrases, and clauses. Is there a different way it could be divided, that would be useful? Explain.

Use the grammar clues to solve this Mystery Sentence:

A four-word simple declarative sentence is one of the most famous statements made by an American civil rights leader. The sentence begins with its subject, a first person singular personal pronoun. The next word is a present tense action verb, which happens to be a word which is often used as a helping verb in the perfect tenses. The sentence concludes with an indefinite article and a subject complement, a singular common noun.

From Kenneth Grahame's

# *The Wind in the Willows*

The Mole was bewitched, entranced, fascinated. By the side of the river he trotted as one trots, when very small, by the side of a man who holds one spell-bound by exciting stories; and when tired at last, he sat on the bank, while the river still chattered on to him, a babbling procession of the best stories in the world, sent from the heart of the earth to be told at last to the insatiable sea.

One of the most profound, if metaphorical, descriptions of a river ever written, this passage from Kenneth Grahame's children's classic, *The Wind in the Willows*, enchants us with its poetry. Look at this passage long and carefully, and see what you can detect about Grahame's art as a writer. What do you notice about the diction? What are the sentence structures? Does he vary the sentence structures?

1. Write a complex interrogative sentence that contains more adverbs than any other part of speech.

2. Write a sentence that illustrates the difference between a direct object and a subject complement.

# Loop Seven Writing Lab:
# The Sentence and the Mind

1. Write a one-page communication that contains no sentences.

2. Read the page to someone, and find out if that person understands what you were trying to communicate.

3. Talk in class about the question, not "why are sentences important to grammarians," but "Why are sentences important to the mind?"

## "Now I must convince him and then I must kill him."

## -Ernest Hemingway

This sentence from Ernest Hemingway's *The Old Man and the Sea* typifies Hemingway's style: short, ordinary words, and a running line that avoids typical clause punctuation in favor of a feeling of interior monologue. The old Man, Santiago, has realized that he must first dominate the fish's will, make the fish believe that he will be caught, and then he will be able to finish the fish.

**Parts of speech**: *Now* is an adverb modifying the verb; *I* is a first person singular subject pronoun; *must* is acting as an auxiliary verb; *convince* is a present tense active voice transitive action verb; *him* is a third person singular masculine gender object pronoun; *and* is a coordinating conjunction that joins two clauses together; *then* is an adverb modifying the verb; *I* is a singular subject pronoun; *must* is an auxiliary verb: *kill* is a present tense transitive action verb; and *him* is a third person subject pronoun.

**Parts of the sentence**: *I* is the subject of the verb/predicate *convince*, which has *him* as a direct object; the second *I* is the subject of the verb *kill* which has the second *him as* its direct object.

**Phrases**: There are no prepositional, appositive, or verbal phrases.

**Clauses**: This is a beautiful, clean, compound sentence. It illustrates why the compound structure exists, rather than there only being the simple option; these two ideas are related, and the second follows from the first. It is more true that they are connected actions, than it is true that they are independent actions. Hemingway flows them together by omitting the expected comma.

## FOUR-LEVEL ANALYSIS

| | Now | I | must | convince | him | and | then | I | must | kill | him. |
|---|---|---|---|---|---|---|---|---|---|---|---|
| **Parts of Speech:** | adv. | pron. | v. | v. | pron. | conj. | adv. | pron. | v. | v. | pron. |
| **Parts of Sentence:** | | subject | | predicate | direct object | | | subject | ----pred.---- | | direct object |
| **Phrases:** | -----no prepositional, verbal, or appositive phrases----- | | | | | | | | | | |
| **Clauses:** | -----------independent clause----------- | | | | | | ------independent clause------- | | | | |
| | compound declarative sentence | | | | | | | | | | |

Identify the **part of speech** in **bold** in each sentence below:

1. The **egocentric** snob didn't notice who he hurt. ____________
2. A paycheck is one of the **tangible** benefits of a job. ____________
3. The **demagogue** played on public prejudices. ____________
4. Don't **preclude** that option. ____________
5. British **cryptologists** cracked the German code. ____________
6. We deplore his narrow **ethnocentrism**. ____________
7. A humorless pedant is a poor **pedagogue**. ____________
8. Galileo was forced to **recant** his heliocentric statements. ____________
9. Permission to travel has been **revoked**. ____________
10. The **pugnacious** bully got his comeuppance. ____________

Identify the *part of sentence* in *italics* in each sentence below:

11. Her **incisive** *questions* cut deeply into the issue. ____________
12. The German leader delivered a ***diatribe*** against France. ____________
13. There is an inexplicable ***anomaly*** in the data. ____________
14. Please **enumerate** your *reasons*. ____________
15. You must *choose* among certain **circumscribed** alternatives. ____________
16. We are *forced* **to intercede** on behalf of the orphan. ____________
17. The **disputatious** reporter irritated the *official*. ____________
18. The **loquacious** fellow wore their *ears* out. ____________
19. We **abrogate** an *agreement* only out of dire necessity. ____________
20. A **prescient** *vision* came to him in a dream. ____________

For each sentence, identify the type of *phrase* in *italics*:

1. It is time ***to advocate** a new policy.* ____________
2. He was crushed by the **ponderous** burden *of the decision.* ____________
3. *Living in fear*, the Gauls expected a brutal **retribution**. ____________
4. The **android's** metallic eye glistened *from across the room.* ____________
5. The crusade *against the **infidels*** was unsuccessful. ____________
6. The **resurgence** *of patriotism* began slowly. ____________
7. She, *a conventional person*, liked his **punctilious** formal conduct. ____________
8. His **condescending** attitude was infuriating *to all of us.* ____________
9. The two **collateral** issues could not be discussed *at one time.* ____________
10. The past, *an eternal mystery*, is **irrevocable** and answers no call. ____________

For each sentence, identify the **sentence structure**. Disregard bold type.

11. Please **elucidate** the matter for our less enlightened guest. ____________
12. Franklin's witty **epigrams** amuse us; we still read them. ____________
13. As time went on, his **eccentric** personality began to moderate. ____________
14. It is wise to be **cognizant** of the laws regulating investments. ____________
15. As I mentioned, the **stringent** regulations seemed severe. ____________
16. The **anthropoid** apes have recognizable facial expressions. ____________
17. Her **diffident** glance caught his eye when she looked up. ____________
18. **Pandemonium** erupted on the playground; it was fun. ____________
19. The diplomat's **urbane** manners set the tone since they left. ____________
20. Because of his spirit, the **tractable** boy was a pleasure to know. ____________

For each of the following sentences, circle the letter of each answer that is true. The answer can be any combination, including all or none. This exercise will teach you the real process of punctuation as a function of grammar.

1. In April she returned and the organization recovered its profits.
   a. a comma after the prepositional phrase
   b. a comma after the dependent clause
   c. a comma after the independent clause
   d. an apostrophe in the contraction
   e. commas before and after the appositive

2. Near Boston Massachusetts the whales avoided Ahabs ship.
   a. a comma after the city
   b. a comma after the state appositive
   c. an apostrophe in the plural noun
   d. an apostrophe in the possessive noun
   e. a comma after the dependent clause

3. A better feeling arose when Stubb the experienced officer walked forward.
   a. a comma to separate the adjectives preceding the noun
   b. a comma before the dependent clause
   c. a comma after the independent clause
   d. commas around the appositive
   e. commas around the noun of direct address

4. Melvilles novel Moby Dick contains a ship named The Pequod.
   a. italics on the ship title
   b. an apostrophe in the possessive noun
   c. quotation marks around the book title
   d. italics on the book title
   e. commas around the appositive

5. The well intentioned remark and the reaction caused thirty five resignations.
   a. a comma between the modifiers that precede the noun.
   b. a hyphen in the compound adjective preceding the noun.
   c. a comma after the dependent clause
   d. a hyphen in the compound number
   e. an apostrophe in the possessive noun

## Yesterday, Jupiter was full and unusually bright.

**Parts of speech**: *Yesterday* is an adverb modifying the past tense linking verb *was*; *Jupiter* is a singular proper noun; *full* is an adjective modifying *Jupiter*; *and* is a coordinating conjunction; *unusually* is an adverb modifying the adjective *bright*; *bright* is an adjective modifying the noun *Jupiter*.

**Parts of the sentence**: *Jupiter* is the subject, and *was* is the linking verb. There is a compound subject complement in the sentence, consisting of the two predicate adjectives, *full* and *bright*. Remember that subject complements go with linking verbs, whereas direct objects go with action verbs.

**Phrases**: There are no prepositional, verbal, or appositive phrases in the sentence.

**Clauses**: The sentence is a simple sentence since it contains only one clause. It is perhaps worth mentioning from time to time that in a simple sentence the entire sentence is the independent clause; all of the words are included in the clause.

• • •

Subject Complements: Here is a compound subject complement. It is a good time to remember the power of subject complements. First, subject complements are very cerebral; many of our strongest ideas, such as Shakespeare's statement that "Life is a walking shadow," involve subject complements. Why? Subject complements let us make equations, saying that A is B, and when A and B are not obviously the same thing at all, this involves a comparison—something that only a person can do. Life is not normally thought of as a shadow, let alone a walking one, and so when Shakespeare used a subject complement form to communicate this idea, he was making an exceptional leap of synthesis.

## FOUR-LEVEL ANALYSIS

| | Yesterday, | Jupiter | was | full | and | unusually | bright. |
|---|---|---|---|---|---|---|---|
| **Parts of Speech:** | adv. | n. | v. | adj. | conj. | adv. | adj. |
| **Parts of Sentence:** | | subject | predicate | -----compound subject complement----- | | | |
| **Phrases:** | no prepositional, appositive, or verbal phrases | | | | | | |
| **Clauses:** | one independent clause, simple declarative sentence | | | | | | |

This sentence beautifully illustrates the binary structure that is the core of every sentence. Every word in the sentence, except the subject noun, is part of the predicate. The subject stands alone, and everything else is about it.

## BINARY DIAGRAM

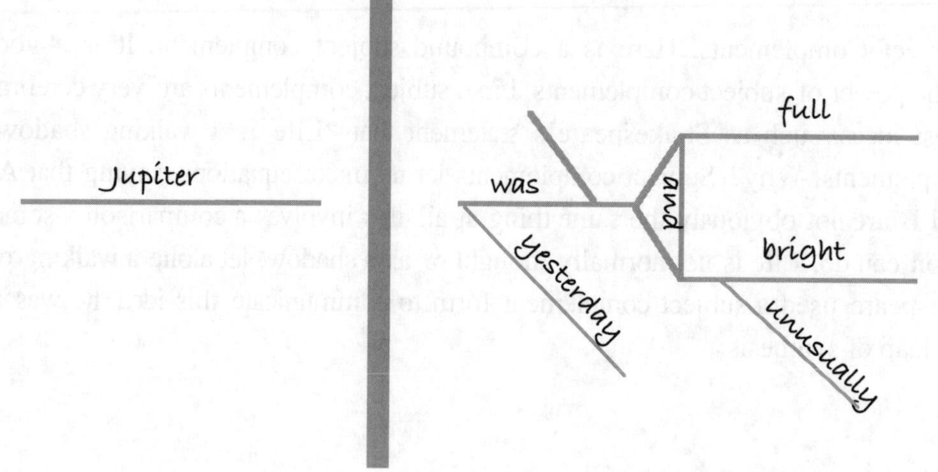

## Questions for individual thought or small group discussion:

**synthesis: making connections**

Think about the word *modify*. We modify a car if we paint it red or alter its fenders. In what sense, if any, is it true to say that an adjective modifies a noun?

**divergence: thinking of alternatives**

How many interesting ways can of think of to organize sentences into a paragraph? Keep thinking until you create new ways that you have never heard of or read about before.

**intuition: ideas from the blue**

Use the following infinitive phrase as the subject of a scary sentence: To turn the key . . .

**emotion: feelings**

Think about how we use punctuation to communicate emotion. How would you punctuate shock, or thoughtfulness, or decisiveness? Could any emotion be punctuated in various ways?

Use the grammar clues to solve this Mystery Sentence:

One of the most famous sentences from the history of warfare in the United States is a simple declarative sentence which begins with a first person singular personal pronoun, then contains a verb phrase in which the verb, which is the first person singular present perfect tense of the verb *to begin*, is separated from its helping verb by two adverbs, then concludes with an infinitive.

From Ernest Hemingway's

# *For Whom the Bell Tolls*

The young man, whose name was Robert Jordan, was extremely hungry and he was worried. He was often hungry but he was not usually worried because he did not give any importance to what happened to himself and he knew from experience how simple it was to move behind the enemy lines in all this country. It was as simple to move behind them as it was to cross through them, if you had a good guide. It was only giving importance to what happened to you if you were caught that made it difficult; that and deciding whom to trust.

Ernest Hemingway's style has been the object of exceptional attention. Look at this passage carefully, and see if you can detect any characteristics that would differentiate Hemingway's writing from anyone else's. Does Hemingway follow the punctuation rules we do? How would you characterize his diction? What do you notice about his use of phrases? Are Hemingway's sentences as challenging to read as some we have seen?

1. Write a compound declarative sentence that contains no conjunction but does contain an appositive phrase and a gerund.

2. Write a sentence that illustrates the use of quotation marks with other marks of punctuation.

# Loop Eight Writing Lab: The Sentence and the Mind

1. Write a paragraph of five sentences or more in which every noun is modified by an adjective and every verb is modified by an adverb.

2. Convert every adjective into an adverb and every adverb into an adjective so that each sentence has at least two incorrect modifiers.

3. Discuss in class the question, "Why can't you make adverbs work as noun modifiers, and why can't you make adjectives work as verb modifiers?"

## "It is so difficult to understand people who speak the truth."

## -E. M. Forster

In his novel *A Room with a View*, E.M. Forster depicts levels of social sophistication that most of us have never thought about. Sometimes his subtle, suave wit reminds us, as in the sentence above, of Oscar Wilde. This sentence seems cynical, but the overall effect of the novel is positive.

---

**Parts of speech**: *It* is a third person singular subject pronoun; *is* is a present tense linking verb; *so* is an adverb that modifies the adjective *difficult*; *to understand* is an adverb; *people* is a common noun; *who* is a relative pronoun; *speak* is a present tense active voice transitive action verb; *the* is an adjective and definite article; and *truth* is a singular common noun.

**Parts of the sentence**: *It* is the subject of the linking verb *is* which links the subject to the subject complement (predicate adjective) *difficult*; *who* is the subject of the action verb predicate *speak* which transfers the action to its direct object *truth.*

**Phrases**: Interestingly, the subject complement *difficult* is modified by an infinitive phrase *to understand people* in which *people* serves as the object of the infinitive; *people* is in turn modified by an adjective clause. We therefore have a clause inside an infinitive phrase.

**Clauses**: This sentence has the feel of a simple sentence, because its dependent clause is buried within an infinitive phrase and obscured by its modification. Since it does not have one clause, however, it is best not to call it simple, but complex.

## FOUR-LEVEL ANALYSIS

| | It | is | so | difficult | to understand | people | who | speak | the | truth. |
|---|---|---|---|---|---|---|---|---|---|---|
| **Parts of Speech:** | pron. | v. | adv. | adj. | --------adv.------- | n. | pron. | v. | adj. | n. |
| **Parts of Sentence:** | subj./pred. | | | subject complement | | | subj. | pred. | | direct object |
| **Phrases:** | | | | | ------infinitive phrase------- | | | | | |
| **Clauses:** | ------------------independent clause------------------ | | | | | | -------dependent clause------- | | | |
| | a complex declarative sentence | | | | | | | | | |

Identify the **part of speech** in **bold** in each sentence below:

1. The quiet boy is an **introspective** loner. ________________
2. We should not **intervene** in their dispute ________________
3. Down's **syndrome** has well-known symptoms. ________________
4. He resented his **subordinate** rank in the military. ________________
5. A **dissonant** clamor arose in the streets. ________________
6. The **belligerent** nations refused to negotiate. ________________
7. It takes money to become a **credible** candidate. ________________
8. "The shadow of **impending** doom" is a trite phrase. ________________
9. Bach's **polyphonic** concertos are beautiful. ________________
10. He wished to be completely **exculpated.** ________________

Identify the **part of sentence** in **bold** in each sentence below:

11. "Rest room" is a **euphemism**. ________________
12. Who was the anonymous **benefactor** to little Pip? ________________
13. A Napoleon complex is a **form** of megalomania. ________________
14. The oil magnates in Saudi Arabia control **billions**. ________________
15. Her vivacious personality cheered **us** all. ________________
16. The heliotropic vines clogged the **window**. ________________
17. There is no **lack** of amour-propre in her! ________________
18. The spry octagenarian won the **race**. ________________
19. This **wine** is preferred by the cognoscenti. ________________
20. He consumed a painful **surfeit** of food and drink. ________________

For each sentence, identify the type of *phrase* in *italics* and give its part of speech:

1. He will quickly **delineate** all *of the options.* ____________
2. *To complicate matters,* the planet moves in a **retrograde** motion. ____________
3. Some people feel a black **melancholy** *on rainy days.* ____________
4. ***Intracranial*** *meditating* will not exorcise her demons. ____________
5. You need **cardiovascular** exercise *to lose weight properly.* ____________
6. The flash was an **epiphany**, *a sudden appearing of insight.* ____________
7. The blue planet, *a gas giant*, reached **perihelion**. ____________
8. Americans possess an **inherent** right *to free speech.* ____________
9. Is the national government a **plutocracy**, *sagging under elitism*? ____________
10. Money, *the* ***sine qua non*** *for acceptance*, was scarce. ____________

For each sentence, identify the **sentence structure**. Disregard bold type.

11. I said that the right/wrong **dichotomy** seemed simplistic. ____________
12. The fascist dictator was a **pathological** liar; he was evil. ____________
13. When we looked, we found a **cryptic** inscription in the stone. ____________
14. He drew an **isosceles** trapezoid on the board, and they understood. ____________
15. The team's careful search did not locate the **pathogen**. ____________
16. As we listened, his **vociferous** protests could be heard for blocks. ____________
17. Please take steps **to rectify** the situation and to make it right. ____________
18. His **sanctimonious** lectures were hypocritical, but no one noticed. ____________
19. The **tortuous** mountain highway wound steeply up as we drove. ____________
20. The insect's **metamorphosis** was miraculous; it was wonderful. ____________

For each of the following sentences, circle the letter of each answer that is true. The answer can be any combination, including all or none. This exercise will teach you the real process of punctuation as a function of grammar.

1. With a rising sense of apprehension my colleague thought Now its time.
   - a. a comma after the prepositional phrases
   - b. an apostrophe in the contraction
   - c. a comma before the direct quotation
   - d. quotation marks around the direct quotation
   - e. a period inside the closing quotation marks

2. When the poet wrote Silver Mune he recalled Jupiter's ancient epic.
   - a. a comma after the independent clause
   - b. an apostrophe in the possessive noun
   - c. a comma after the dependent clause
   - d. italics on the poem title
   - e. quotation marks around the poem title

3. A one third minority chose batteries cables and connectors.
   - a. a hyphen in the compound adjective
   - b. a colon at the beginning of the list
   - c. a comma after the plural common noun
   - d. a comma before the coordinating conjunction
   - e. a comma after the dependent clause

4. Pausing suddenly the venerable grizzled sailor realized its identity.
   - a. a comma after the prepositional phrase
   - b. a comma between the adjectives preceding the noun
   - c. a comma after the participle phrase
   - d. a comma after the gerund phrase
   - e. an apostrophe in the contraction

5. Pensar is the Spanish verb for think it is a common verb.
   - a. quotation marks around the Spanish verb
   - b. italics on the Spanish verb
   - c. a comma after the independent clause
   - d. a comma after the dependent clause
   - e. a semicolon after the independent clause

## Attacking and withdrawing are unpleasant alternatives.

**Parts of speech**: *Attacking* is a noun (a gerund); *and* is a conjunction (a coordinating conjunction); *withdrawing* is a noun (also a gerund); *are* is a present tense linking verb; *unpleasant* is an adjective modifying the plural common noun *alternatives*.

**Parts of the sentence**: The sentence has a compound subject composed of two nouns joined by a coordinating conjunction: *Attacking and withdrawing*. The verb *are* is a linking verb which links the compound subject to the subject complement *alternatives*; *alternatives* is a subject complement because it renames the subject—it completes the subject. The point of a sentence containing a subject complement is to tell what the subject is, not what the subject does. It is a question of identity.

**Phrases**: There are no prepositional, gerund, infinitive, participle, or appositive phrases. There are two individual gerunds, *Attacking* and *withdrawing*, but neither gerund has complements or modifiers attached to it. A gerund, as this sentence shows, is a noun that ends in -ing. One way to know that the word is a gerund and not a verb is to understand that -ing verbs must have helping verbs with them: ***have been** attacking*, ***will be** withdrawing*, etc.

**Clauses**: The sentence contains only one clause, so it is a simple sentence. The subject/predicate set is *Attacking-withdrawing/are*.

## FOUR-LEVEL ANALYSIS

| | Attacking | and | withdrawing | are | unpleasant | alternatives. |
|---|---|---|---|---|---|---|
| **Parts of Speech:** | n. | conj. | n. | v. | adj. | n. |
| **Parts of Sentence:** | -----------compound subject---------- | | | predicate | | subject complement |
| **Phrases:** | no prepositional or appositive phrases; compound gerund as subject | | | | | |
| **Clauses:** | one independent clause, simple declarative sentence | | | | | |

## BINARY DIAGRAM

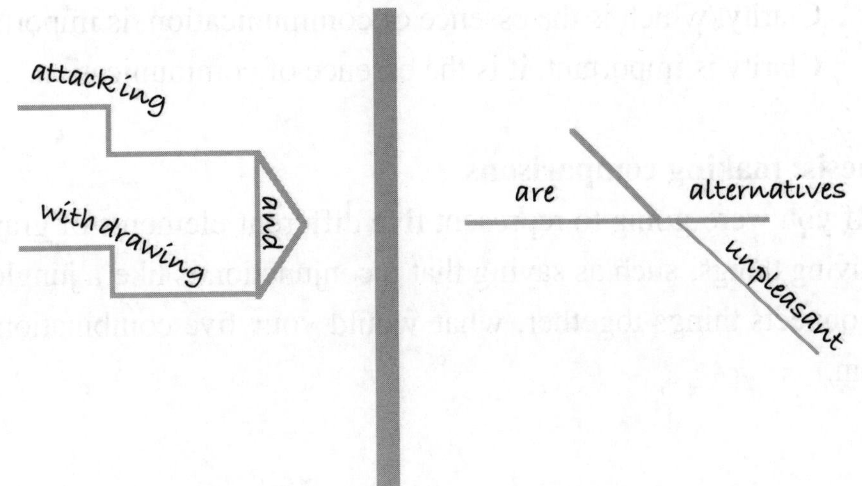

**Questions for individual thought or small group discussion:**

**analysis: breaking down into components**

We call *to be*, *to do*, *to dance*, etc., infinitives. The word *infinitive* contains the ancient pieces *in*, meaning without, and *fin*, meaning limit. In what sense are infinitives without limit? What limit are they without?

**evaluation: judging value with criteria**

In a compound sentence, two or more independent clauses (ideas) are shown to be related, and the compound structure implies that each idea is of equal value. In a complex sentence, the idea in the subordinate clause is understood to be of a lower (sub) order (ord) of importance than the idea in the independent clause, though the ideas are still related. With this in mind, which is better:

Clarity, which is the essence of communication, is important.

Clarity is important; it is the essence of communication.

**synthesis: making comparisons**

If you were going to represent five different elements of grammar with living things, such as saying that a conjunction is like a jungle vine that connects things together, what would your five combinations be? Explain.

Use the grammar clues to solve this Mystery Sentence:

A sentence from a fairy tale begins with a proper noun of direct address, used twice, followed by an imperative independent clause containing an understood subject, a present tense transitive verb, an adverb, a second person singular possessive pronoun, and a singular common noun as a direct object. All words are one-syllable words except for the noun of direct address, which contains three syllables.

From Marjorie Kinnan Rawlings's

# *The Yearling*

A clear space opened at the creek's bank. Jody saw a vast black shapeless form break through. Penny Halted and lifted his gun. On the instant, a small brown missile hurled itself at the shaggy head. Old Julia had caught up with her enemy. She leaped and retreated, and in the moment of retreat, was at him again. Rip darted in beside her. Slewfoot wheeled and slashed at him. Julia flashed at his flank. Penny held his fire. He could not shoot, for the dogs.

This passage, from Marjorie Kinnan Rawlings's *The Yearling*, describes how Jody, his father, and their dogs fight with Old Slewfoot, the bear in the Florida swamp. What characterizes the sentences in this passage? Why?

1. Write a complex sentence that contains a gerund, a participle, and an infinitive, but has no prepositions.

2. Write a compound sentence with two semicolons and a comma.

# Loop Nine Writing Lab
## Appositive Phrases

1. Write a paragraph about a famous individual, in which you mention various other famous individuals, and be sure to insert a brief appositive phrase after the first mention of each individual's name, so that the reader will know who each person is. It would be good if you also mention various objects and places that need clarification with appositives. Use as many appositives as you can to clarify everything for the reader.

2. Rewrite the paragraph so that it contains all of the same information, including all of the information that was in the appositives, except this time, do not use appositives. Do it some other way.

3. Compare the two versions of the sentences.

4. Write a statement that explains the use and benefit of appositives.

## "I contracted for it; I earned it; it was paid to me."

## - Frederick Douglass

Although Frederick Douglass worked to earn money, his slave owner took the money away; it was one of the great indignities that Douglass resented and that motivated him to seize his own freedom. His *Narrative* is among the greatest works of American literature.

---

**Parts of speech**: *I* is a first person singular subject pronoun; *contracted* is a singular past tense intransitive action verb; *for* is a preposition relating its object, the pronoun *it*, to another word in the sentence, in this case the verb; *I* is a singular subject pronoun; *earned* is a past tense transitive action verb; *it* is a third person singular object pronoun; the third *it* is a third person singular subject pronoun; *was paid* is a passive voice past tense action verb; *to* is a preposition; *me* is a first person singular object pronoun. This sentence puts *it* through all its paces; we see *it* as the object of preposition, as the direct object, and as the subject of a verb!

**Parts of the sentence**: *I* is the subject of the verb *contracted*; *I* is the subject of the verb *earned*, and *it* is the direct object of *earned*; *it* is the subject of the passive voice action verb *was paid*.

**Phrases**: Two prepositional phrases: *for it* modifies contracted, *to me* modifies *was paid.*

**Clauses**: This compound declarative sentence contains three clauses in only eleven words, and uses semicolons to make a chain of I;I structures. The first clause is *I contracted for it*; the second clause is *I earned it*; and the third clause is *it was paid to me*.

## FOUR-LEVEL ANALYSIS

| | **I** | **contracted** | **for** | **it;** | **I** | **earned** | **it;** | **it** | **was** | **paid** | **to** | **me.** |
|---|---|---|---|---|---|---|---|---|---|---|---|---|
| **Parts of Speech:** | pron. | v. | prep. | pron. | pron. | v. | pron. | pron. | v. | v. | prep. | pron. |
| **Parts of Sentence:** | subj. | pred. | | | subj. | pred. | direct object | subj. | ----pred--- | | | |
| **Phrases:** | | | -prep. phrase- | | | | | | | | -prep. phrase- | |
| **Clauses:** | ---------indep. clause---------- | | | | ----indep. clause----- | | | ---------indep. clause------- | | | | |
| | an I;I;I compound declarative sentence | | | | | | | | | | | |

Identify the **part of speech** in **bold** in each sentence below:

1. His **chronic** illness dragged on for years. __________
2. His colorful **hyperbole** livened his conversation. __________
3. Dr. King's **sonorous** voice echoed over the crowd. __________
4. Her **germane** comments really hit the mark. __________
5. His **convivial** friends loved to celebrate. __________
6. His **cognomen** is "Huckleberry." __________
7. The **anarchist** passed out leaflets to passersby. __________
8. Your **animadversions** on his behavior are superfluous. __________
9. The deliberate snub was a low, **pusillanimous** act. __________
10. The mayor ducked a question with a clever **subterfuge**. __________

Identify the *part of sentence* in *italics* in each sentence below.

11. Her **saturnine** personality won *her* few friends. __________
12. *They* were forcefully **expatriated** from the fatherland. __________
13. Flagpole sitting is a highly **sedentary** *occupation*. __________
14. Ishmael was a popular *fellow* of appealing **bonhomie**. __________
15. The company will make a **bona fide** *offer*. __________
16. The wealthy **bon vivant** lived the good *life*. __________
17. The **mutable** *laws* of high fashion can't be predicted. __________
18. It is *unnecessary* to **impute** evil motives to opponents. __________
19. It can be *dangerous* to disrupt the **status quo**. __________
20. The incident offers an instructive ***paradigm*** for future guidance. __________

For each sentence, identify the type of *phrase* in *italics*:

1. The debate created a **schism** *in the Democratic Party.* ________
2. His **bootless** effort *to win acceptance* was pathetic. ________
3. *Seized with enthusiasm*, the media created the champ's **apotheosis**. ________
4. The rumblings were the **precursor** of what was *soon to come.* ________
5. Dyslexics sometimes **transpose** letters *in a word.* ________
6. The Prime Minister, *a veteran*, endured her opponent's **invective**. ________
7. The origin of atoms, *a* ***cosmological*** *question*, is unknown. ________
8. His **effusion** *of officious greetings* made us wince. ________
9. It was bittersweet *to present a* ***posthumous*** *award.* ________
10. Mole loved the **euphony** *of the wind in the willows.* ________

For each sentence, identify the **sentence structure**. Disregard bold type.

11. The **refractory** child broke and rebroke the rules. ________
12. We need fresh ideas; we do not need hollow **platitudes**. ________
13. He began to feel **acrophobia**, but he didn't have xenophobia. ________
14. When they first arrive, some visitors feel **agoraphobia**. ________
15. Notice the fable's eerie **verisimilitude** if you can. ________
16. We even loved his many **idiosyncrasies**. ________
17. The government chose to regard the act as **casus belli**. ________
18. The nation survived a peaceful **interregnum**, but it didn't last. ________
19. As you will see, it was an unintentional **infraction** of the rules. ________
20. He will receive a **condign** punishment for his offense. ________

For each of the following sentences, circle the letter of each answer that is true. The answer can be any combination, including all or none. This exercise will teach you the real process of punctuation as a function of grammar.

1. Hail Marching Legions is the song to sing if its a new invasion.
   a. italics on the song title
   b. quotation marks around the song title
   c. a comma before the dependent clause
   d. a comma before the independent clause
   e. an apostrophe in the contraction

2. Yes its mandatory to include three objects in a two dimensional plane.
   a. a comma after the interjection
   b. an apostrophe in the possessive pronoun
   c. an apostrophe in the contraction
   d. a comma after the independent clause
   e. a hyphen in the compound adjective

3. In the Great Dismal Swamp the outbreak of malaria is up by one third.
   a. a comma after the introductory prepositional phrase
   b. a hyphen in the fraction
   c. a comma after the dependent clause
   d. commas around the appositive
   e. commas around the parenthetical remark

4. On September 11 2009 Smithers our ablest engineer designed the new bridge.
   a. a comma after the day
   b. a comma after the year appositive
   c. a comma after the participle phrase
   d. commas around the appositive
   e. a comma after the dependent clause

5. Caught in the blue tube Tashtego reached for the harpoon.
   a. a comma after the dependent clause
   b. a comma after the introductory prepositional phrases
   c. a comma after the participle phrase
   d. commas around the appositive
   e. a semicolon between the clauses

## As the doomed mansion burned, she tried desperately to escape.

**Parts of speech**: *As* is a subordinating conjunction; *the* and *doomed* are adjectives modifying the singular common noun *mansion*; *burned* is an action verb; *she* is a third person singular pronoun (We don't know the antecedent.); *tried* is a past tense transitive action verb; *desperately* is an adverb modifying the verb *tried*; *to escape* is an infinitive verbal noun.

**Parts of the sentence**: *mansion* is the subject of the verb *burned*, and the pronoun *she* is the subject of the verb *tried*; *to escape* is the direct object of *she/tried*. Neither clause contains a subject complement or an indirect object.

**Phrases**: Neither clause contains a prepositional phrase. There are also no participle phrases, gerund phrases, or infinitive phrases. We do see a single participle (verb form used as adjective), *doomed*, though it has no complements or modifiers to form a phrase. We also see an infinitive, *to escape*, which also lacks the required complements and modifiers to make a phrase. So in this sentence the infinitive is simply the direct object of the second clause, and not an infinitive phrase.

**Clauses**: This complex sentence contains two clauses. The first clause, *As the doomed mansion burned*, is a dependent clause, because it makes no sense by itself. This clause clearly needs (depends on) an independent clause to complete its meaning. This dependent clause begins with a subordinating conjunction, *As*, which is enough to make the clause dependent (It subordinates the clause). Notice that if you remove the subordinating conjunction and let the clause read *The doomed mansion burned*, the clause makes sense and is then an independent clause.

The second clause in the sentence, *she tried desperately to escape*, is an independent clause. The subject is *she*, and the verb--or simple predicate—is *tried*. Since the independent clause comes last, we put a comma between the clauses.

• • •

Escape? Yes, the heroine did escape! We're thinking here of images from *Gone with the Wind*, which later inspired countless novels and films.

## FOUR-LEVEL ANALYSIS

| | As | the | doomed | mansion | burned, | she | tried | desperately | to escape. |
|---|---|---|---|---|---|---|---|---|---|
| **Parts of Speech:** | conj. | adj. | adj. | n. | v. | pron. | v. | adv. | n. |
| **Parts of Sentence:** | | | | subject | predicate | subject | predicate | | direct object |
| **Phrases:** | no prepositional or appositive phrases; an infinitive as direct object | | | | | | | | |
| **Clauses:** | one independent clause, simple declarative sentence | | | | | | | | |

## BINARY DIAGRAM

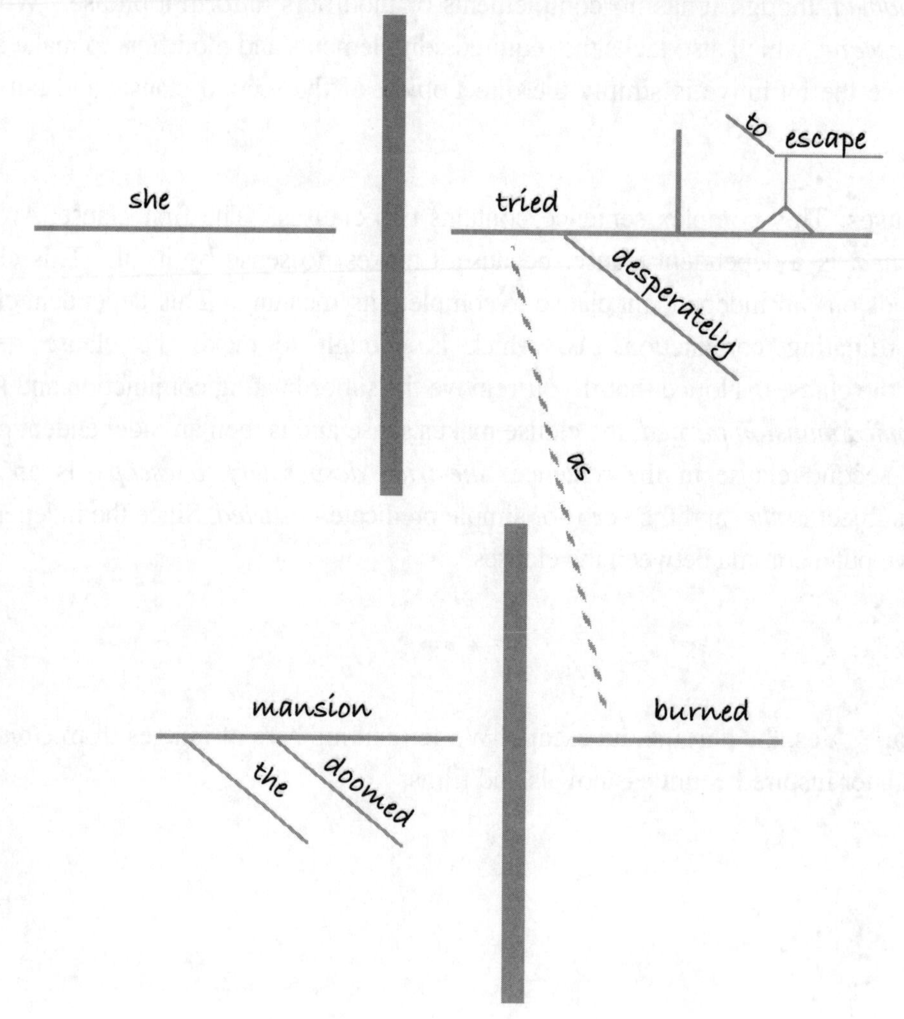

**Questions for individual thought or small group discussion:**

**synthesis: making connections**

What grammatical structure do you think most resembles an algebraic equation?

**divergence: thinking of alternatives**

How many true statements can you make about indirect objects? Think about this question until the obvious answers are exhausted, and you produce some answers that are interesting.

**intuition: ideas from the blue**

In a dream you hear a series of sharp imperative sentences, followed by a subject pronoun. What are the words, and what is happening?

**analysis: breaking ideas into components**

There are eight kinds of words, but how many groups do these eight kinds make? Explain your analysis.

Use the grammar clues to solve this Mystery Sentence:

A famous sentence by Franklin Roosevelt begins with a definite article and an adjective both modifying a singular common noun which is the subject of the clause. This subject is then modified by an interrupting adjective clause containing a first person plural subject pronoun, a present tense action verb, and an infinitive used as an adverb. The main clause then concludes with a present tense linking verb a singular common noun, and a reflexive pronoun.

From George Eliot's

# *Silas Marner*

Even people whose lives have been made various by learning, sometimes find it hard to keep a fast hold on their habitual views of life, on their faith in the invisible—nay, on the sense that their past joys and sorrows are a real experience, when they are suddenly transported to a new land, where the beings around them know nothing of their history, and share none of their ideas—where their mother earth shows another lap, and human life has other forms than those on which their souls have been nourished.

George Eliot's real name was Mary Ann Evans, but in her time, brilliant women found it difficult to be published, and so Evans took *George Eliot* as her *nom de plume*. How many sentences are there in this passage from the beginning of the second chapter of George Eliot's classic novel? What is the subject/predicate set of the main clause? What are the advantages of the style Eliot uses in this passage?

From Edgar Allan Poe's

# *The Tell-tale Heart*

But even yet I refrained and kept still. I scarcely breathed. I held the lantern motionless. I tried how steadily I could maintain the ray upon the eye. Meantime the hellish tattoo of the heart increased. It grew quicker and quicker, and louder and louder every instant. The old man's terror *must* have been extreme!

Study this passage from Edgar Allan Poe's classic short story carefully, and see if you can explain how the sentence structures change with the content. Can you see why what you are describing could dictate the way you make your sentences? Should Poe have shortened this? What words should he have removed?

1. Write a sentence that has a gerund as a subject, a gerund as a direct object, and a gerund as a subject complement.

2. Write a sentence of ten or more words that has an unmodified common noun as a subject, and that has only one clause.

# Loop Ten Writing Lab
# Modification

1. Write a descriptive paragraph about a unique scene; it could be a scene at the ocean, in the mountains, or in a storm—something vivid and unusual.

2. Revise the paragraph, removing all adjectives and adverbs, and replacing the nouns they modified with more specific nouns if you wish. Try to get the same effect and detail without using any modifiers.

3. Compare the two versions of the paragraph.

4. Write a statement explaining what you learned about the effect of modification.

# "Either that wallpaper goes, or I do."

## Oscar Wilde

There are times when it is best to think before issuing an ultimatum, as in the case of the last words that Oscar Wilde ever spoke, "Either that wallpaper goes, or I do." Analyze the grammar of Wilde's fatal epigram.

**Parts of speech**: *Either/or* is a correlative conjunction used to join two clauses together; *that* is a demonstrative adjective modifying the singular common noun *wallpaper*; *goes* is a present tense action verb; *I* is a singular first person personal pronoun; and *do* is a present tense action verb. Both *goes* and *do* are intransitive.

**Parts of the sentence**: The subject/predicate set of the first clause is *wallpaper/goes*, and the subject/predicate set of the second clause is *I/do*. Since there are no linking verbs, there are no subject complements, and a glance shows there are no direct objects, either. If there are no direct objects, there can be no indirect objects.

**Phrases**: The sentence contains no prepositional, verbal, or appositive phrases.

**Clauses**: The sentence is a compound declarative sentence in which the clause *that wallpaper goes* is joined to the clause *I do* by the correlative conjunction *Either/or*.

## FOUR-LEVEL ANALYSIS

| | Either | that | wallpaper | goes, | or | I | do. |
|---|---|---|---|---|---|---|---|
| **Parts of Speech:** | conj. | adj. | n. | v. | conj. | pron. | v. |
| **Parts of Sentence:** | | | subject | predicate | | subj. | pred. |
| **Phrases:** | no prepositional, appositive, or verbal phrases | | | | | | |
| **Clauses:** | two independent clauses, compound declarative sentence | | | | | | |

These were the last words of Oscar Wilde!

Identify the **part of speech** in **bold** in each sentence below:

1. They had a private **colloquy** in the corner. __________
2. Is the fetus mature enough to be **viable**? __________
3. Here is a brief **synopsis** of the course. __________
4. The argonauts longed to stand on **terra firma** at last. __________
5. We cannot **sanction** the use of our name. __________
6. The editor was an unapologetic **Russophobe**. __________
7. The doctor presented a **prognosis** of the disease. __________
8. We purchased a large **polychrome** sculpture. __________
9. Her deeds of **philanthropy** were legendary. __________
10. Everyone admired the **perspicacity** of her mind. __________

Identify the *part of sentence* in *italics* in each sentence below:

11. The text showed the ***mobocracy*** of the revolution. __________
12. The Soviet **gerontocracy** is losing *control.* __________
13. His **magniloquent** oratory was *impressive*. __________
14. The police tried *to arrest a **kleptomaniac***. __________
15. Her ***joie de vivre*** was inspiring. __________
16. The *school* must act **in loco parentis**. __________
17. The thinker was *reluctant* to deal with **mundane** matters. __________
18. He gave a refreshing, **unequivocal** *answer*. __________
19. The icy ***nihilism*** of his mind could be unnerving. __________
20. He paid *one* of them an **invidious** compliment. __________

For each sentence, identify the type of *phrase* in *italics* and give its part of speech:

1. *To increase accuracy*, science uses a process of **induction**. ______________
2. *Governed by fear*, the Iranian **hagiocracy** banned swimsuits. ______________
3. The pedant confined himself *to a scholarly Latin* ***diction***. ______________
4. Johnson, *the* ***disconsolate*** *widower*, missed his wife. ______________
5. *His* ***disingenuous*** *offering* of assistance fooled the ingenue. ______________
6. The **fractious** mob clamored *to avenge the outrage*. ______________
7. The mendicant, *a plaza regular*, wore a **nondescript** garment. ______________
8. The **prolific** writer wrote seven books *in two years*. ______________
9. We read the novel, *a* ***chronicle*** *of the brave knight-errant*. ______________
10. *Crushed into stone*, coal is the remains of a **primeval** forest. ______________

For each sentence, identify the **sentence structure**. Disregard bold type.

11. The speech was a **panegyric** on her talent; it was effective. ______________
12. Your task is to read Dante's **magnum opus**, the *Divina Comedia*. ______________
13. He loved grandfather's **antediluvian** ideas, and he took his advice. ______________
14. We need to process a customer's request **expeditiously**. ______________
15. The **decadent** century saw little greatness in art as we have seen. ______________
16. His arrogant, **supercilious** manner offended everyone. ______________
17. It is true; her **inexorable** fate followed her everywhere. ______________
18. When dawn broke, they greeted an **emissary** from the Queen. ______________
19. The **improvident** spendthrift went broke, but he recovered. ______________
20. As I said, the **moribund** corporation fired half its work force. ______________

For each of the following sentences, circle the letter of each answer that is true. The answer can be any combination, including all or none. This exercise will teach you the real process of punctuation as a function of grammar.

1. In May the ship reached its darkest moment when a tsunami struck.
   a. a comma after the prepositional phrase
   b. a comma after the month
   c. an apostrophe in the possessive pronoun
   d. an apostrophe in the contraction
   e. a comma between the clauses

2. As the heat wave abated Queequeg leered at the shipmate.
   a. a comma after the participle phrase
   b. a comma after the dependent clause
   c. a comma after the independent clause
   d. a semicolon between the clauses
   e. a comma after the prepositional phrase

3. The double braced hull is tight caulked and dry.
   a. a hyphen in the compound adjective
   b. a colon before the list
   c. a comma after the adjective **tight**
   d. a list comma after the adjective **caulked**
   e. a comma between the clauses

4. Swimming among the whales was the expatriots deepest desire.
   a. a comma after the introductory participle phrase
   b. a comma after the dependent clause
   c. an apostrophe in the possessive noun
   d. commas around the appositive phrase
   e. commas around the parenthetical remark

5. Yeah the expedition found twenty five whales beyond the outer reef.
   a. a comma after the introductory adverb
   b. a comma after the interjection
   c. a comma after the dependent clause
   d. a hyphen in the compound adjective
   e. a comma before the prepositional phrase

# Grammar Review Test

## Preparation Notes

In addition to questions on all of the Four-Level Analysis sentences from the beginnings of the loops, the Grammar Review Test contains a section of questions on clause punctuation. Students will be presented with sentences they have never seen before, and they will be expected to identify the clause structure, determine what punctuation is needed, and show where the punctuation should go. A thorough review of the notes on clause punctuation and identification is in order.

Students should be reminded that on a given question, more than one answer may be true; they should pick the *best*, most complete, answer.

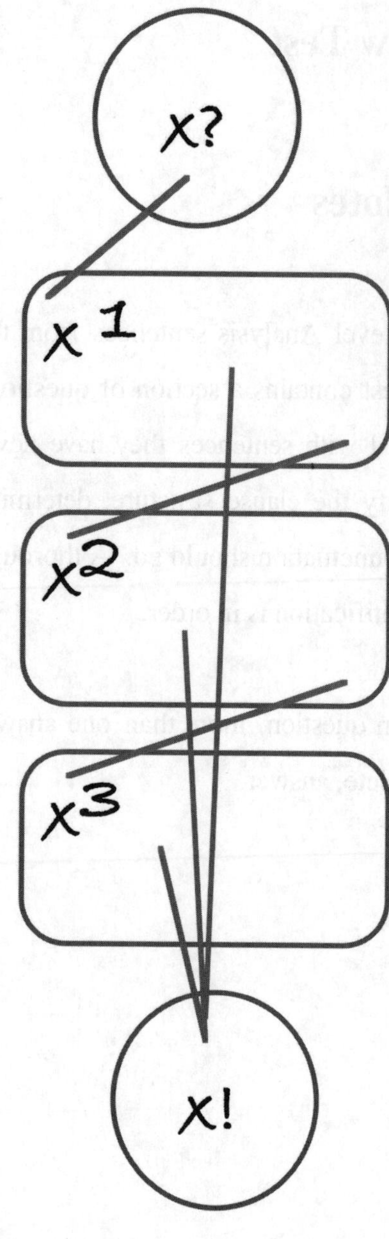


Simplicty

An essay
is about one thing.
Introduce it, develop
your case for it in
several ways, and
then conclude it.
Maintain focus
with consistent
key words, and by
devoting every
paragraph to the
one thing.